SEA OF DREAMS

SEA OF
DREAMS

THE SELECTED WRITINGS OF

GU CHENG

TRANSLATED, WITH AN INTRODUCTION,

BY JOSEPH R. ALLEN

A NEW DIRECTIONS BOOK

Book design by Sylvia Frezzolini Severance
Manufactured in the United States of America
New Directions books are printed on acid-free paper.
Published simultaneously in Canada by Penguin Books Canada
First published paperbound by New Directions in 2005

Library of Congress Cataloging in Publication Data

Gu, Cheng, 1956-
[Poems. English Selections]
Sea of dreams : the selected writings of Gu Cheng /
translated, with an Introduction by Joseph R. Allen.
p. cm.
ISBN 0-8112-1587-3 (alk. paper)
I. Title: Selected writings of Gu Cheng.   II. Allen, Joseph Roe.   III. Title.
PL2874.C492A6 2005
895.1'152—dc22

2004028186

New Directions Books are published for James Laughlin,
by New Directions Publishing Corporation.
80 Eighth Avenue, New York 10011

Table of Contents

Introduction by Joseph R. Allen   vii

THE EARLY POEMS (1964–1979)   1

AN ANCIENT BOAT (1980)   5

DRIFTING DRIFTING (1981)   21

BULIN'S FILE (1981–1982)   35

WIND DREAMS (1982)   47

I DREAMT OF FISHES (1983)   61

EULOGY TO THE WORLD (1983–1985)   77

OVER THE BORDER (1984–1988)   97

LIQUID MERCURY (1985–1988)   103

SEA BASKET BLUES (1989–1991)   127

TWO SEQUENCES (1992)   137

THE CITY: A DREAM SEQUENCE (1991–1993)   151

EPILOGUE (September 1993)   177

SELECTED PROSE   179

Index   203

Introduction

by Joseph R. Allen

In October, 1993, readers across the world were shocked when they heard that one of China's most celebrated contemporary poets, Gu Cheng, had assaulted his wife and then hanged himself, leaving her to die in the hospital a few hours later.[1] He was thirty-seven years old; she was thirty-five; their son was five. Some would see this as a desperate act by a romantic and naïve genius who had been victimized and abandoned by the women he loved; others would see it as the final event in a life of an immature, self-obsessed impostor who had taken advantage of those around him. Gu Cheng had always been seen as an eccentric figure in the contemporary literary scene; with his death everyone seemed to take sides—he was either a child of nature or a monster. I have no intention of entering that debate, but I do want to trace the connections between Gu's life and his art. Gu Cheng's peripatetic life mirrored the dramatic changes in Chinese society in the late twentieth century. Both personal and political changes contributed to the range, richness and variety in his work.

LIFE AND WORK

Gu Cheng's literary career rose from the ashes of the Cultural Revolution and contributed to the reawakening of lyricism in China during the 1980s. Born 1956 into privilege, if not wealth (his father was a well-known writer and party member), Gu Cheng during the early years of his life in Beijing must have been relatively comfortable. A family anecdote captures those youthful days:

> One night after dinner, the family went out for a walk together. As he walked along, Gu Cheng looked up at a large willow tree that stood on the side of the road and said, "Losing an arm, I open wide an eye." Father was sort of startled by this; he laughed and asked Gu Cheng if the tree preferred to have an eye or an arm? Gu Cheng, who seemed to be suddenly shocked by the thought, did not reply. After returning home, he worked on the poem, asking his older sister how to write the characters. The poem was saved by his mother [and became one of the first two poems in his collected works].[2]

Here one senses that the young Gu Cheng was surrounded by a devoted and attentive family: father as critic, sister as tutor and scribe, and mother as anthologist. As well as their child, he seems to be their literary project.

That world quickly shattered however. When he was twelve, Gu Cheng accompanied his family to the barren reaches of Shandong province, where they had been "sent down" when the Cultural Revolution cranked up its anti-bourgeoisie machine. While not the harshest of treatments of those troubled times, this exile reduced their lives to that of peasants, and ended Gu Cheng's formal education. It is here we get the seminal vision of natural innocence to which Gu Cheng clung throughout his life. Viewed in retrospect, the years in Shandong become a haven for innocence: "He was all alone, only able to commune with selfless nature; in this way he escaped from the turmoil of the human world."

Gu Cheng's discovery of this "selfless nature" is one of the most common tropes in the construction of his aesthetic sensibility; he says that he learned poetry from the natural world, direct and unmediated: from raindrops, lavender, and hermit crabs (see his "Poetry Lessons"). Later, it would be dreams, hallucinations, and visions that functioned as this extra-literary engine. This is, of course, simply a conceit used to characterize his disenchantment with the everyday world; "art is made of art" and Gu Cheng no doubt learned much about writing poetry from other poetries. (During this time he was fascinated with a nineteenth-century book of entomological drawings, one of their few cultural possessions; indeed, the line drawings that he produced throughout his life have a bizarre, illustrative, natural-history quality to them: like scientific drawing seen through a kaleidoscope.) In terms of poetry, I think we can assume two early influences: classical Chinese poetry and his father. Classical poetry is central to the ubiquitous culture of memorization in China, which helps explain why the popular mind generally conceives of it as "poetry." We witness Gu Cheng's early familiarity with this poetry in the small corpus of classical-style poems he wrote, as in this example from his first year in Shandong when he was thirteen:

> You, sir, walk the dike midstream
> the two banks white with frozen snow
> A spring wind brushes across one's face
> and spring waters in torrents flow[3]

The structure, language and affective scene of this occasional vignette makes for a respectable version of classical Chinese poetry, characterized by a merging of the mundane scene with the mental world of an "I" narrator. We wonder if perhaps the classical "sir" (*jun*) refers to his father? That would make sense, since, in many ways, the stories that come from those years are "father and son" tales—they were said to have herded pigs together during the day, writing poems in the sand, and on scraps of paper to be burned in the cooking fire so that "only flames were their readers."

In 1974 that pastoral idle gave way to a life in the city when Gu Cheng and his family moved back to Beijing. Like many of the "educated youth" sent down to the countryside, Gu Cheng had to learn to live in a radically altered world: he became an urban laborer and budding intellectual—carpenter, house painter, illustrator, and editor. He writes:

> I hail from reedy beaches of the north
> I left, following
> the graying road, to enter
> a city crammed with gear wheels
> into narrow alleys
> and wooden shacks, each lowly heart
> in a swirl of smoke, cold and remote

In 1976 he participated in the Tian'anmen demonstrations, which jump-started a new youth culture in China focused on "democracy" and from which the underground journal *Today* was born. In late 1978 he was befriended by a group of somewhat older writers associated with that journal. Later, he, along with other *Today* poets, became identified with a new poetry, called *menglong* by the critics—a term commonly translated as "misty," but whose meaning is closer to "hazy." This poetry offered an ambiguous, symbolic, and introspective literary vision to young readers who were bone weary of decades of simple didacticism, or what Gu Cheng called "rhyming editorials"—see his "Misty Poetry: An Interview." Sometimes this new poetry was filled with political innuendo; sometimes it offered the reader only an essential, slightly ambiguous, imagistic moment. The best combined the two. Gu's small lyric of 1979, "A Generation," became the slogan for his time:

> Even with these dark eyes, a gift of the dark night
> I go to seek the shining light

The early 1980s were heady days for the young people of China as the country emerged out of decades of social dislocation and political lunacy toward a promise of freedom, comfort, and stability. These were Gu Cheng's most prolific years; he frantically wrote poem after poem, sending them out over the country for publication in the emerging literary venues. He writes: "It was like being a real poet—on the road with a group of editors from *The*

Poet magazine. We swaggered through the streets, bullshitting with each other and looking for a bathroom." In just a few years, Gu Cheng rose to become one of China's celebrity personalities, instantly recognizable in his signature stove-pipe headwear—a leg cut from a pair of jeans. It was a time when everyone was reading and discussing the new literature, especially the "misty poetry." Celebrated and censured in a range of popular and official media, the poetry captured the "shared journey, shared reality, and shared ideals" of the lost generation of young people of China. For the older generation, including Gu's father, it was a poetry that was just "too difficult to understand." The young writers in Beijing became "rock stars" of China, with fans that cut across all social groups; they were Springsteen, Sting, and Paul Simon, all in one, performing their poetry to adoring crowds. The central government even dispatched them into the countryside on good-will visits where "the guests from on high were treated not just as deities descending to earth, but even as the Kitchen God returning to his palace in heaven."

In the 1990s, after the brutal events of June 4th, 1989, the lyricism of the post-Mao era gave way to a more mercantile, jaded urban society, where television replaced newspaper boards and cell phones replaced poems. Political dissent was suppressed or traded in for material goods of a consumer culture that emerged from the economic reforms of the 1980s. By the time of the June 4th mayhem, Gu Cheng was already living abroad enjoying an international reputation; yet he also faced personal demons as he struggled to re-establish the simpler times of his life. Following visits to Europe, the United States, and Hong Kong, Gu Cheng and his wife, Xie Ye, moved in 1987 to New Zealand where Gu taught Chinese at the University of Auckland. He had entered a new type of isolation, living in an international society which he could not easily communicate with or understand—he never learned any other languages despite his long residences in Europe and New Zealand.

Then in 1988, he and Xie Ye bought a small, dilapidated house on an island in Hauraki Gulf off the coast of Auckland. Here they took up an impoverished Thoreau-like existence with their newly born son: sort of a self-imposed "sending down." The house, which is featured undisguised in his novel, *Ying'er*, became nearly an obsession for Gu Cheng. Of their first night there, he writes:

> Lei [Xie Ye] wrapped the baby in a small blanket and placed him on the only sofa we had, and then she got down to work. That night was filled with wind and rain and we lit a candle. I looked at Lei and said, "This is the place I have been looking for for twenty years. I have been looking for it ever since I left school when I was twelve."

And later in a poem, he wrote about a brighter day: "Listen/ this house is our sunshine."

Their friend and the object of his infatuation, Li Ying, joined them on the island in 1990:

> I had dreamed about it so often, and then finally she got her passport. On the telephone I listened to her speak softly about getting the passport, the flights, the visas. Her voice seemed different. I looked at Lei; she seemed somewhat hesitant, but then quickly agreed to buy the airplane ticket.

Thus began the *ménage à trois* that haunts his novel and much of his later poetry. In the novel that is spelled out in graphic terms: "All I had to do was thrust a little, and she would cry out in pleasure." In the poetry, things come to us through a lyrical filter that veils the occasion of the work:

THE SOUND OF A WINDOW OPENING

You hear
the sound of a window opening
in the distance is the sea

        The glistening boat
        lies in the dunes
        in the distance   is the deep blue sea

Listen
that whisper you hear   is sound of the sea

        The boat lies in the dunes
in the distance stretches the deep blue sea

This relationship became the fodder for much of the critical literature that appeared after the couple's death. That criticism, both positive and negative, plumbed his poetry for the currents of death that became so clear in hindsight. Yet, what really is significant about Gu Cheng's later poems is their deepening complexity, which stands in such contrast to the search for a simple life on his island. It is as if the island were a physical defense against the complex emotions impinging on him. In the end, even the house seemed to have turned on him; a few months before he died he wrote to a friend:

When you read my book [*Ying'er*] you will know how completely sick I am, only my hands are normal. I have spread pieces of our ruined garden everywhere, spread pieces of myself everywhere. See how the world has meant so little to me, but so much to her. I want to preserve those times together in that white cottage; she abandoned it, and so did I. The cottage did me harm. I should not have left Beijing in the first place; I should not have lived so long. The most beautiful days should be those just before the end.

His life on the island—and the poetry produced in those years—seems to have been complicated by two seminal events: the Tian'anmen tragedy in 1989, and the couple's return to Germany in 1992-1993. The massacre in Beijing, when the hopes of the 1980s came crashing down, haunted Gu Cheng's dreams throughout the following years, almost as if he suffered from a "survivor's guilt." At the same time, the months he spent in Berlin broke his moorings to house and home—Li Ying remained behind on the island, but left with another man before Gu Cheng returned. These tensions, and even the mental anguish, seem to have produced the best of his poetry, as it struggled to draw his innocence and experience together. This complexity is best seen in the long poetic sequences occupying the last part of his corpus, especially "The City: A Dream Sequence." Of this, he wrote:

In my dreams I often go back to Beijing, but it has nothing to do with Beijing of today. It is a place that is heaven-sent just for me. Peace Lake and China Gate are now gone; also gone are the bricks in the bright sunlight, the cinder road along the hillside, and the wild jujube trees. And yet, I still move above them, looking down on all below and on days to come.

In this sequence, originally titled, "The City: June 4th," Gu Cheng creates a bewildering nostalgic pastiche of his old city, his friends, and the tragedy that befell them, all filtered through the medium of his recalled dreams.[4]

We should not think, however, that Gu Cheng was completely consumed by angst during those final years. In both his letters and his poems we find moments of the old, untroubled innocence: at the very end, he writes to his parents, "By nature I am not a happy person, but right now I am very much at peace, just playing with Little Chubs and his toy cars . . ." This was also the time when he wrote the playful prose-poem sequence "Classical Tales," which is filled with puns and written in tongue-in-cheek faux-classical Chinese. It begins with the island, the sea, and a slight hint of tragedy:

The lord of the island dwells on his isle, scanning the skies. In days past he bid his time in the mountains, yearning for the sea. Then, quite unexpectedly, above the South Pole the ozone layer was breached, and, with the melting of glacial peaks, the ocean waters rose. Thus came baleful bother to the one of his desires.

ON TRANSLATION AND LANGUAGE

In the earliest stages of Chinese literary criticism there is a canonical formula of poetics: *shi yan zhi*: "poetry puts into words that which occupies the mind," or more simply, "poetry verbalizes intent."[5] Ignoring for the moment the problem of how phenomena come to "occupy our minds," this formula asks us to see poetry as "translation," in which one strives to represent psycho-phenomena in language, which in turn becomes what "occupies the mind" of the reader. Thus, we can place literary translation at the end of a chain of such representations; it is a translation, another representation, of what "occupies the mind," but this time, that of the reader, not of the writer. While I recognize the generative status of phenomena that become a writer's occupation, when we translate we are unlikely to be able to recover/represent those phenomena because they are already veiled behind a series of representations formulated within the limits of language. Rather we are likely to translate more accurately our own occupations, which we share in our immediate contemporary condition. Discussions with my collaborators, Zhang Jing and Chou Changjen (both highly competent and informed readers) often focused on what "occupied their minds" when they read these poems, instead of what might have been Gu Cheng's intent.

Through the two decades of his writing, Gu Cheng explored the possibilities of language to represent the emotions that seemed to take possession of him, his *zhi*. In general, he worked within a relatively simple vocabulary and mode of presentation. While there are important exceptions, such as his prose poems in the "Classical Tales" sequence, Gu Cheng's language is usually relatively mundane and his presentation much in the psycho-affective *shi yan zhi* mode. Gu Cheng is indeed very concerned about "what occupied his mind."

Experimentation in language of Gu Cheng's early poems is primarily in terms of substitution by metaphor. While the images and the metaphors in these poems are often new and fresh, even bizarre, the language itself remains relatively commonplace. We might note that this writing in "substitutions" was a social-political condition of the times—the highly euphemistic language of the Great Leap Forward and Cultural Revolution began that newspeak, which required readers to decipher daily messages of the government-controlled media. (Some sense of this language is seen in Gu's satirical pieces "With a TV Mounted on the Wall" and "Eating at Desert Creek.") In his poetry Gu Cheng exploits that method by writing in metaphorical language that straddles the political and personal, the mundane and the mythical. His most famous epigraphic poems (such as "One Generation" and "Impression") are obvious examples of this use of the single metaphor to represent the coming together of the mental and phenomenal world. Rhyme and rhythms in these poems are also rather simple and direct, as "Generation" and "Impression" attest. Translating this language into English presents no great obstacles, although adjustments are always necessary. In my experience these adjustments are most often necessary in interrupting the commonly repetitive language, which works better in Chinese than English (often working for more assonance and alliteration in its place), and in toning down the sentimentality of the poems, which often comes with an emotional climax in the closing lines of the poem or stanza; in English these seem to strike rather false notes.

In Gu Cheng's later and longer poems these metaphors are often extended, either by agglutination or elaboration. The "agglutinative poems" string out a series of metaphors in relatively unintegrated layers, while the elaborative poems draw the metaphor out into a conceit of its various manifestations. The two most common extended metaphors of Gu Cheng's early and middle poems are those of the sea and the dream (or fantasy), which have suggested the title for this volume of translations. In the most complex of these extended metaphors we have long, integrated constructions, such as in "Life's Fantasy" and "Wind Dreams." At the extreme, these extended metaphors yield the early poetic sequences, both of the elaborative and agglutinative kinds, such as "An Ancient Boat" and "Eulogy to the World." The "Bulin's File" sequence uses these techniques within an extended narrative, producing a very special set of poems. The challenges and opportunities in translating these sequences are necessarily multiplied but not substantially different from those in the shorter poems.

As we move into the later poems we sense that the metaphor, epigraphic or extended, can no longer fully represent what is occupying Gu Cheng's mind. In these poems, fragmentation of the language sets in and the tentative logic of syntax and metaphors begins to implode. This is accompanied by his diminishing use of punctuation and the increasing use of the broken and elliptical line structure.

Chinese language lends itself to this type of syntactic manipulation. The lack of number, inflection, and tense allows for a wide range of indeterminacy in the relations between words. This is particularly so in poetic forms that tend to weaken the word-order dependent grammar of Chinese—if your object, for what ever reason, floats away from its syntactic position in the sentence, there is no way for it to maintain its "case." On one level this means that the Chinese reader does not sense ambiguity in the same places as the reader of English—since there is no marked tense, a verb that can refer to past, future and present actions is not ambiguous unto itself. This ambiguity should not be translated, or at least not given special notice. Yet on another level it is clear that Gu Cheng's later poems exploit the particularities of Chinese language to create conspicuous ambiguity—that is, an ambiguity that needs to be translated.

Small signs of this fragmentation are visible even in the early, simpler metaphors where imagistic disjuncture is introduced (eyes for arms, dark eyes seeking light, colors in the grayness). This disjuncture spreads slowly throughout the later poems along with two new complexities: one at the syntactic level, and the other at more multiple levels. With syntactic fragmentation come non-sequitur structures in verse and stanza. Different readings seep away in two directions from a given phrase, such as in "Sea Basket Blues." The more fragmentary poems, such as "Walled Dreams, and an Awakening," interweave the agglutinative metaphors with this fragmentary syntax to become highly disruptive. While the vocabulary of these poems remains relatively unadorned, they are wracked with juxtapositions defying semantic integration, sometimes appearing to be a jumble of words on the page—words are sometimes even fragmented within themselves, such as when two characters of the fixed binome for "sala/ mander" (rong/ yuan) are separated on adjacent lines in his "Ghosts Enter the City" sequence. Often we sense that we are listening to broken and half-heard conversations; as if we were indeed listening to a dream. Translating the language of these more disruptive, playful poems has been the special difficulty (and pleasure) of my work.

The most important task of any translator is to find a voice for the poet in the translated language; one has to imagine what the poet would have sounded like if he or she had written in that other language. Of course, we do not want to "translate away" the distinctiveness of Gu Cheng's poetry; we need to hear the language, rhythms and constructions that are distinctly his, but in this case, as manifested English. Only then can we be part of the chain of representations that began back in the first step of *shi yan zhi*.

ACKNOWLEDGEMENTS AND SELECTIONS

This volume of translations, *Sea of Dreams*, has been from the beginning a collaborative effort, with several individuals each contributing in essential and distinct ways. It began in 1998 with Zhang Jing, my former student in Comparative Literature at Washington University in St. Louis. We focused our attention on the post-1988 poems and produced a complete translation of them. Zhang Jing, a life-long fan of Gu Cheng and resident of Beijing, not only helped with that translation, but also provided background details, especially for "The City: A Dream Sequence." A large number of poems from that early work have been included here, some with further revisions.[6] Chou Changjen, my tutor from the International Chinese Language Program at National Taiwan University, provided insight and consultation on all the pre-1988 poems, prose selections, as well as the post-1988 poems. Her extensive background in classical and contemporary Chinese literature was extremely valuable to this process. Zhou Danlong, my longtime friend and reader, reviewed and critiqued the translations as I worked through their several versions, especially in the last few months. As a writer and artist himself, Zhou always provides special insight and sharp criticisms, for which I am always grateful. In the final stages of the work, Declan Spring of New Directions and Eliot Weinberger made numerous helpful suggestions and corrections. I especially appreciate Eliot's suggestion to include all the major sequences and Declan's gentle guidance through the expansion of the book. Throughout the translation process, Gu Xiang, the older sister of Gu Cheng, provided valuable advice and information about the poems and other texts. Finally, none of this could have been completed without the support of the College of Liberal Arts, University of Minnesota, and the facilities of the Loft Literary Center, which is part of the Open Book in Minneapolis.

The selection of poems in *Sea of Dreams* is based largely on Gu Cheng's own *Selected Poems*, published in 1993, shortly before his death.[7] I have deviated from his selection by including the poetic sequences that he mentions (p. 230) but did not include in his own selection, as well as his last sequence, "The City: A Dream Sequence," which was published posthumously.[8] If there were discrepancies between different versions of a poem, I followed his *Selected Poems* and the emendations provided by Gu Xiang. This includes the poems' punctuation and line structure. The addition of prose works, which range from letters to selections from his novel, *Ying'er*, should help give a sense of the full range of Gu Cheng's literary styles. Finally I have included a few of the line drawings that accompany his "Classical Tales" sequence. This has produced a volume that is substantially longer and more varied than Gu Cheng's own *Selected Poems*, but one that, I believe, still represents his intentions.

1   There is much debate about what actually occurred that day; a variety of interpretations are found in Li Xia's *Essays, Interviews, Recollections, and Unpublished Materials of Gu Cheng* (Lewiston, NY: Edwin Mellen, 1999). Here can also be found a wide range of assessments of Gu Cheng's life and work.

2   This anecdote is attached to Gu Xiang's on-line version of *Gu Cheng's Complete Poems*, see www.gucheng.net.

3   *Zoule yiwanyiqianli lu: Gu Cheng shoudu mianshi shishougao* (Walking the 11, 000 Mile Road: Gu Cheng's Poetry Manuscripts). Gu Xiang, ed. (Beijing: *Shiyue wenyi*, 2005), p. 28.

4   Wolfgang Kubin (in "Gu Cheng: Beijing I," in *Essays, Interviews*) discusses the sequence and gives detailed notes (his own, and those taken from Gu Cheng) on the meaning of several of the poems. The title "The City: June 4th" is from his materials; Gu Xiang (on-line Notes) gives the alternative title, "The City: A Day in June."

5   This expression dates from ca. 600 BC, and becomes closely linked to the earliest Chinese poetic work, the *Book of Songs* (Shijing) in commentaries dating from around 100 BC. The phrase has received a great deal of attention in the study of Chinese poetics; Stephen Owen's treatment *Readings in Chinese Literary Thought* (Cambridge: Harvard East Asian Studies, 1992) is the most sophisticated and detailed in English.

6   A portion of the 'Classical Tales from Waiheke Island" sequence was first published (with Zhang Jing) as "From 'Classical Tales from the Isle of Waves: Eighteen Poems with Illustrations' " *in Parnassus*, 25, 1-2 (2001): 380-83.

7   *Gu Cheng xinshi zixuanji: Hai lan* (The Self-selected New Poems of Gu Cheng: Sea Basket Blues) (Tianjin: *Baihuawenyi*, 1993).

8   Besides these major additions, certain other earlier poems were added, especially ones that were well-known and/or from Gu Cheng's own list of "representative poems." Some poems from his selection were not translated since they did not work well in English.

The Early Poems

1964–1979

WILLOW BRANCHES

Losing an arm,
I open wide an eye.

DUSK

The hard north wind
blows away our faded footprints;
the sun slides down behind the mountain,
the world is like a giant paper-cut in silhouette.

SMOKESTACKS

The smokestacks stand like giants tall on the level plain
looking out over the world flooded with lamp light,
chain smoking cigarettes
they ponder things beyond our comprehending.

MY FANTASIES

I fantasize,
and fantasies disintegrate;
fantasies forever forgiving their disintegrations,
but disintegrations never setting those fantasies free.

LIFE'S FANTASY, A TUNE

Place these dreams and fantasies,
in a long and spiral shell.

1

Willow branches woven for an awning,
while the song of the summer cicada turns round and round.
With halyards tightly drawn,
and wind lifting the sails of morning mist,
I will put out to sea.

There is no purpose in this,
just bobbing under the blue sky,
letting the cascade of sunlight
wash over me and darken my skin.

Sunlight is my tracker.
It pulls me along
with a line of intense light.
One step at a time.
It trudges twelve hours, a journey to the end of the day.
I am pushed by the wind,
eastward, and westward,
the sun melts into evening.

Dark night comes
and I sail into the bay of the Milky Way.
Thousands of stars watch
as I drop
the crescent moon—my golden anchor.

The sky begins to lighten,
and the sea teams with icebergs of dark clouds
Shifting and colliding.
The rumble of thunder, lightning's flash!
Where will I go from here?
The universe is too endless.

Weave a cradle
from golden stalks of wheat,
and place inside it
thoughts and inspiration.
With this carriage securely yoked,
let time set out
sending greetings to the world.

Its wheels rumble through
the growth of thyme and chrysanthemums.
Crickets welcome me,
with their lute strings trembling,
my hopes melt into blossoms.
Deep night is like a mountain valley
and daytime its peak.
To Sleep! I close my eyes,
and the world is no concern of mine.

The quarter horse of time
drops from exhaustion.
The yellow-tailed waxwing
makes her nest inside my carriage.
As always, I want to travel the world on foot
off to deserts, forests, and their remote corners.

The sun bakes the planet
round like a loaf of bread.
Barefoot,
I go walking on,
leaving footprints behind
like seals stamped across the earth,
and the world too melts
into my life.

I want to sing
of humankind,
a song that will resound forever
through the universe.

YOU AND I

You should be a field of dreams,
and I should be a gust of wind.

ONE GENERATION

Even with these dark eyes, a gift of the dark night
I go to seek the shining light

COMING HOME

As night slides out of its dark mountain cave,
the setting sun waits, gazing toward the horizon.

It casts a long floating shadow
toward the quiet village.

The old man and his ox return home,
pulling an ancient cart behind them.

An Ancient Boat

1980

GRASS SHACK

The wick's bright flame
comes to life again
wind blowing through the cracks
cannot put out its light

Under the table
the cat is stalking something
no butterflies now
just moths fluttering in the night

SNOWMAN

I built a snowman
at your front door
to stand in my stead, waiting there
in all its stupidity.

Then you buried your lollipop
deep into its snowy heart,
saying this little sweetness
would perk it up.

The snowman did not smile,
did not make a sound,
and then the bright spring sun
came to melt him away . . .

Where is he now?
Where is that candied heart?
A bee buzzes
beside the small puddle of tears.

MARTYRED

Stand still!
Yes, I will. I now have no reason to flee.
For me, this is the end of the road,
even though my hair is still black
and life has really yet to begin.

The small elm stands there a stranger;
But the white-flowered bush is so familiar.
Earth, mother earth
I'll listen to your song,
never naughty again, never again . . .

Perhaps my companions will come searching
but they'll not find me, I am well hid away.
All that is piled like building blocks
in the fields beyond the city
secretly amazes me.

Wind, don't hide away,
this is a time to celebrate, a new beginning;
I have lived my life, and happy
now I quietly accept
this gift, so generous.

LAKE COUNTRY

On a clear spring day made for picnicking
the pale purple wind
trembles—
dissolving the confusion and the clamor
the flowered tablecloth
and that tune with its greasy stains . . .
this is a village in the lake country
to which I come, walking softly
with breath flowing like silk
with my damp shadow
bright yellow canola flowers
dandelions and goslings

all steal away
with my footprints

I know that
you sleep there peacefully
beneath thin,
finely mortised tiles
where canopied boats come to moor
around you lay old songs
and toys
—the spiked helmet of bamboo shoots
the imprints of bricks
in the pottery bowl where duckweed floats
fish lie still
a beetle in the small bamboo tube
bursts into chirping
the cloud like grandma
draws the curtains
your little dark-skinned Hindu brother
is yet to be born . . .

I hear
the praise of birds and leaves
the saw's steady rhythm
the song of oars
the arching melody of rainbow bridge and orchid leaf
and, at the edges of the earth,
wind's soft query
I feel
the trembling green wheat
the smooth glide of the river's current
and the brimming fragrance
rising from the trays of blushing fields
oh, South
what can I say
such is your childhood
such is my dream

. . .
Yes, you love to laugh
even though you're not awake

have you found the stars
fallen between the cracks in the floorboards?
that dense gnarl of wood
removed and
turning into a fountain of flower and mist
the north wind and the tides of the eastern sea
swirl slowly round
within your silver collar
is this your father's long-winded story
or your mother's
feeling that is not to be explained?

You have gone away
like some thin wisp of smoke
passing through the living room, with its gleaming tiles
through the gaps between the rounded stones
through the stands of shy and slender bamboo
no footprints
no footfall
just door after door like piano keys
sounding softly with the pulse of sighs
. . .
I know now
that I have two lives
one has not yet ended
and the other has just begun

In your brief dream
I walk on
walk along every route, in every direction
walk on toward the forest
stepping into the villages of mushroom tribes
walk along twisting branches and winding roads
leap over the cleverly rolling hills
Walk on toward sandbars
on toward thoughts as wide as a river
and toward poems woven of brambles
hiding out in beehives and bird nests
I walk on toward the old collapsing pagodas
chimneys, and the antennae of high-tension lines
seeping through the mountains and hills

—a warrior's heart
sinks into the ocean
a never ending kiss . . .

And when you awake
everything has changed
everything so tiny it frightens you
reality is nothing more than
spider webs and the tiny claws of crayfish
holding on to last night's rain, its remaining drops
ripples of a dream . . .
I
will return
have returned
climbing that flight
of warm and shaded stone steps
climbing the round table
and base carved of basalt
beyond, just beyond the small bamboo door
a world
waits for you

PARTING GIFT

A thousand times, at least
I've read those words of parting
and a hundred times
I've seen such scenes
and yet we, today
you and me,
are the ones about to step over
that high and ancient threshold

No well-wishes then, no good-byes
all that is but a performance
better to keep silent
to conceal is not to lie
let's leave behind old memories, gifts to the future
just as one might give dreams to the night
tears to the ocean
and wind to the sails on the evening tide

AVOIDING EVERYTHING

You don't want to plant flowers
because, you say, "I don't want to see them
wilt and fade."

So
to avoid the ends of things
you avoid all beginnings

NEAR AND FAR

You
glance up at me,
then glance off toward the clouds.

I feel as if
you're looking at me from afar
and at the clouds from nearby.

A GAME

Was it yesterday? Or the day before?
Well, it was in the past, that's for sure
that we wrapped a handkerchief around a stone
and threw them both high into the blue sky—

Such a frightening, dizzy feeling
the earth and sky spinning round
we let go with our feverish hands
and waited for God's harsh judgment

But there was no thunder, no lightning
only the stone falling silently back to earth
and what of the accompanying handkerchief?
there, caught high in the top of the trees

Since then, we've not seen each other
as if traveling on, further and further on
only that single, faithful stone remains behind
in silence, longing for its companion

IMPRESSION

Gray sky
gray road
gray buildings
in the gray rain

Through this wide dead grayness
walk two children
one bright red
one pale green

CLINGING VINES

Your handkerchief fluttered down
from the balcony above
the blue sky hiding its smile
I used a bamboo pole to return it to you
"thanks," you said,
black bangs caressing the white clouds

From that time on
I planted climbing vines
grapes, honeysuckle, and wisteria
clinging to bamboo poles
taking hold of balcony railings
waiting for you to come again

But someone says you've moved away
who says? A dream
so why is there still that blue sky
with white clouds silently sailing by?
Small butterflies white in the flowers
floating down and rising up again

Later, I see some guy
some freckle-faced stranger
leaning against the railing of the balcony
whistling
he plucks a grape
and says, "Yuck, how sour"

ALONG A STREET

A crowd of people dancing
along a street I've never seen before
they dance wildly but with precision
so I cannot cross to the other side

With all this waiting, and waiting
I have become a street sign
pointing toward my own destination
without a word of explanation

JUST A BIT OF HOPE

I am piled here
with countless other pebbles
like eggs that will never hatch

The clear blue water creeps in
to swallow us up
and silently spit us out again

I hope for no more
than that the grass will be able to lengthen
its shadows

THE WARMTH OF A WINTER DAY

A raven lands
in the winter trees
as black as night before pre-dawn's light
so black it shines
first one eye, then the other
behind it stands the silent, cloudless sky

A feeling of warmth
an expanding constraint in the midst of warmth
forces me to leave
treading along loose gravel
in the scattered shadows

why are there so few tadpoles
swimming, reconnoitering the green coral

AN EVASION

Through the towering boulders
I walk
toward the sea

"Speak to me," I say,
"for I know all the languages of the world"

The sea smiles
and reveals to me
birds that swim
and fish that fly
and beaches that can sing

Yet, it utters not a word
in response to that undying question

OFFERING COMFORT

These grapes, green and wild
small, pale and yellow moons
mom worries
how to make a jam of them

Don't add any sugar
I say
there's already a drop of sun
sweet and red
on the morning fence

NEAR THE SEA OF DREAMS

Near the sea of dreams
so many close companions
silent without a word
have premonitions of some lurking danger

A strange child
marches forward through the breeze
stepping onto the rocks, with no good intentions
walking toward the beach

There a small boat
enticed by the wet sounds of love
takes on a thousand different postures
trying to break free of its mooring line

MY RÉSUMÉ

I am a child of grief
never grown up
I hail from reedy beaches of the north
I left, following
the graying road, to enter
a city crammed with gear wheels
into narrow alleys
and wooden shacks, each lowly heart
in a swirl of smoke, cold and remote
I continue on with my green stories
believing in my audience
—the open sky, and
spray off the tops of waves
these will someday cover me completely
covering too that lost
grave; I know
that then all the flowers and grasses
will gather round
and in the glimmer of the fading lamplight
kiss lightly my grief away

I'D RATHER DIE
— From a crumbling cell on death row, the hero addresses his enemy

Don't waste your breath
I'd rather die than give in

Although I would miss this life
with its vegetables and fields of rice
and I would miss having a silver room
in which to store the sunlight
I would miss too the window sill
layered there with sun-drenched flowers
and autumn's maple leaves
And I would miss
watching songbirds
fly my heart up to the eaves

Don't waste your breath
I'd rather die than give in

Although I long for love
and to travel miles more
seeking that path
among pointless clouds
and I long to use the light touch of a kiss
between the forest and the windows
to place pollen on her eyelashes
walking along the lullaby
toward my youth
saying goodbye to streetlights

Don't waste your breath
I'd rather die than give in

Although I need my freedom
just as a blade of grass
wants to slough dirt off its body
just as the sunflower
seeks its own crown
I need the open sky
a stretch of blue, washed clean by breezes
to let my lines of poetry slowly
like ripples
spread their fruits and grains

Don't waste your breath
I'd rather die than give in

AN ANCIENT BOAT

1.

Waves convey life
convey all
the sunlight that resists its own sinking
the spreading warmth in my palm
makes me move on
leaving the sky and the sea
to go off to meet kind shoals and
weird reefs
passing through narrow straits—the parted lips
of two continents draw near
in the shortest of nights
presenting each hopeful heart, one by one
to waiting eyes

2.

Full of curiosity, the sea lion
swims in from polar regions
and behind it a lovely tiger shark
its rippling stripes looming larger
the octopus in a panic retreats
and frightened minnows sparkle in agitation
only the barnacles hold steadfast to their love
with teeth bared inside their sweet kisses
and all
I can do is to wait silently
with pride and humility
for their hatred and rejection

3.

I know the mood of the sea
and know the reasons for its tolerance
warm inky currents
stream out from its coral beds
with an invitation to clear cold waters
to go off and dance together

self reflections, countless and mysterious
come into being and die away
both undulating and stolid lives
generation after generation sinking into stone
using the designs of their own skeletons
to decorate time
creating symbols of oceanic memories

4.

Banks of rich and luxurious clouds
sweep in from the edge of the sky
hems of silver light slipping into line
beneath this proud, pompous rank
I raise my sails
raise my searching hands
but this is not to beg of them
for they cannot hold
my attention
rather I inquire
of those thin but true winds
who come in from the forests
with news of my companions

5.

Yes,
I remember my old companions
pines, red and white, standing straight and tall
all crowded together beside high mountain lakes
gazing down on birds in flight
and singing the same song
ancient rays of moonlight
all becoming little children
with new mushrooms solving riddles in green dreams
yes, perhaps you'll party wildly for a lifetime
until lightning strikes
in this disaster you will rise up to heaven's kingdom
but in my misfortune I'll sink to the bottom of the sea

6.

Perhaps I'll go peacefully
into old age
taking my leave of these demanding waves
and guided by tangled tow lines
sail a river deep into the interior, with loving looks
perhaps there is some small shoal
where I can lie face down in the sand
and let the sun burn away my rheumatic pain
perhaps then a couple of world-weary lovers
will come quietly by
and arrange the marbled stones
to raise me up
and take their rest under my cover

7.

In the rain storm, limp and paralyzed
lying in a puddle, lined with sand and pebbles
the thin thread of kitchen smoke tells the sky
tells all life related to the sky
that I'm a roof
I'm still sailing on
but what I transport now is not hopeful spices
rather fruit grown round and ripe in the land of fortune
I'm sailing between heaven and the sea
mooring at the shore of life
naked children spill out from the windows and doors
jumping into the sunlight
and begin playing with the scuttling crabs

Centuries ago a small boat sailed up the River Seine. Exhausted, it moored on the shore of a small island midstream in the river.

Life was easy on that small island, so a small fishing village was born—a village with the name Lutèce, with cottages on the river.

Paris was a child of these cottages on the river. Never forgetting its past, the crest of Paris bears that boat sailing across the waves, with its sails raised high.

WE GO SEARCHING FOR A LAMP

We've walked so far
searching for a lamp

You say
it's behind the window shade
encircled by the pure white wall
wildflowers moving in from the sunset
will change into some other hue

We've walked so far
searching for a lamp

You say
there it stands on the small platform
gazing out at the dried fields all around
letting the railroad cars move quietly by
carrying memories of gentleness and warmth

We've walked so far
searching for a lamp

You say
there it is on the shore of the sea
beautiful like a kumquat
and all the adoring children
will grow old in the morning

We've walked so far
searching for a lamp

NEW YEAR'S EVE

The song of tattered paper panes
has ended
no rippling in the glass

The bridal chamber sinks into a dark red dream

The cat stares out
and so does the dog
with steam hovering
over their soft backs

And above the haystacks hangs one shining star

Drifting Drifting

1981

RETURNING HOME

Don't fall asleep, not now
dear one, for the road is still long
don't lean too close to temptations of the forest
don't lose hope

With water cold from melted snow
write this address on your hand
or lean on my shoulder
as we pass through the mists of early morning light

Once we raise this transparent storm
we'll be home
a round patch of grass
spreading out beside the old pagoda

There I will
guard your weary dreams
chasing away the flocks of dark nights
leaving behind only the sun and bronze drum

And on the other side of the pagoda
small ocean waves
stealthily climb the beach
collecting together the trembling sounds...

A CREVICE

A crevice
the slight neglect of stone and boards
seduces
the voyeur's gaze

the sound of the revolver turning round
the bead holding its breath

The springtime calls out
seeds seek their sunlight
a centipede
snaps like a chain, and disappears

A crevice

TAKE THIS BRANCH OF BLOSSOMS

Since it's plucked already
take this branch of blossoms, please
as you go along your road
faintly pressed there in the sea of hardened sand

Let the wind blow when it will
petals down
let the road of stars
fly off into the open skies

And finally, please go toward the altar
a little closer
turning round this branch in your hand
go and wait for that glimmer of light

EARLY SUMMER

As the dark clouds slowly thin
I leap from the moon's round window
leaping over stretches
of still and lovely water
returning to the village

On the new mud wall
sprouts of green grass grow

Each wooden door
new

clean and pure as the acacia flower
the paper windowpanes soundless
like empty white envelopes

Don't believe me
and don't believe the others

Slip the still sleeping
forget-me-nots, two by two,
into the round door knocker
let all stories begin
each filled with fragrance and surprise

Dawn comes
climbing quickly into the tops of the trees

I shed my straw hat
shed that familiar shell
and turn into
a light green katydid
and yes, I'll call katydid, katydidn't

The rooster is aging
with faded feathers hanging down

All those little girls early to rise
go to the woods beyond the fields
to pick spring's last
red cherries
and smile too

THE HARVEST

Tired, yes so tired
behind us, sheaves of wheat quietly sleep
let us too close our eyes
softly kissing and
drinking from the spring

Clouds round and full float across the open sky
one, then another

We can go now
with our dull sickles in hand
go off to grasslands that lie green beyond the fields of wheat

DRIFTING DRIFTING

No longer a shoreline
no longer street lights

Everything waves and whitecaps

The existence of a continent
is only some legend now

I just want to stop and rest
but fear I will sink and drown

RAIN

Raising our colorful placards toward the sky
we protest against this sort of sorrow

GRASSLANDS

The pitch-black grasslands
melt away
staining the transparent wind

Still the moonlight is clean and sparkling

Gathered together by this perplexity
the flock of silver sheep
do not move a bit

Let me look at you

How can your eyes
be such strangers to me
in a night so familiar

SPRING HAS NOT YET COME

Spring has not yet come
the branches are still black and bare
but we must leave each other now
to close down this loneliness of ours

When I turn, turn the last time, and look
I see something green there
the collar of your coat
flapping lightly in the wet wind

I go walking on
along whatever road
until I am swallowed up
by the waves of young wheat

HERE, WE CAN'T REALLY GET TO KNOW EACH OTHER

Here
we can't really get to know each other
there are walls
endless lamps, and searching stares
appraising us
(and if we shut the door to the world outside
then we are prisoners within)

We should run away
no, it should be an abduction
I'll be the bandit
making off with you
like some rainstorm raging over hills and fields

When we have gone and disappeared
leaving behind only the sound of our breathing
you'll walk there
suddenly looking up at me
and then down at the ants frantic in the dew
their jet-black heads
glinting with rainbows

SELF-CONFIDENCE

You say
you no longer put faith in destiny
or in the evidence of fingerprints
with your small fist raised high
you no longer believe in anything

Squinting
you cross the leaf-strewn road alone
surprising those winds of leisure
behind your back

Proudly you walk on
all decided now
walk on
as if behind you
came a small child
so depressed that he cannot even cry
called fate

THE ANCIENT WAR

Horseshoes and decorated swords glint in the sunlight
tassels and ribbons on helmets flutter in the gunfire

Death
the glory of death is what everyone needs
the rites for the fallen
are more exciting
than those for God

The troops are arrayed
standing together
they raise their sacred banners
and trumpets sound the charge

This, only to make mothers weep
and to make children proud

I'M A CRIPPLE NOW

I'm a cripple now
I cannot go for a stroll
I cannot go
with the one I love
or go with all the strange shadows
off toward the morning light

I'm a cripple now
I cannot hop over stones
or hop over the brook that babbles on
to go off to see those fretting plums
and those lovely flowers
with blue eyes

I'm a cripple now
everything passes me by
lights like bees swarming to a new hive
and night and day
black and then white
like zebra stripes

I'm a cripple now
I must remain behind
but I cannot even stand
beautiful like a sapling
I have no hopes of green
or of growing tall

I'm a cripple now
but still I smile
my smile is the freedom
of a cloud
or of a herd of deer
bounding off to some place far away

THE VERY LAST TIME

For the last time
for the very last time, I've awoken

curtains pushed aside
sunlight sparkling like silver hair
dandelions dancing
in the young wind
falling and filling my bookcases

My name is over there
as I meticulously pave the path
with pebbles of poems
forever glittering tears
a pond of dreams
with the forest in its reflection
having shed its green fatigues

Perhaps there are also songs
many of them
built with joy of
buttercups and orchid bells
my little friends
run there
in pursuit of a black terrorist butterfly

Now, I shed everything
shed my world
and very lightly, a paper boat
riding the waves of the dark sea,
slowly comes to the edge of the bed
and I depart
floating off into eternal space

FOR MY GRAVE

I will not need flowers
for my grave
nor sighs, nor sobs
I'll need only a few aspens
to stand there happy and tall
like brothers
a swath of grass green in the wind
among shadows of sun and cloud
in the ever-changing light

DISCRIMINATIONS

I'm tired of walking
walking into the late autumn
fallen leaves flooding the temple yard
cover me
but I would so much like to stumble
into the hubbub
sinking into the eternal sea

I want so much to love you
until our bones turn white
hand in hand
traveling toward the gray, drizzling rain
holding hands
quietly until we turn into skeletons
in the end a visitor will come
a bird made of mud
to sing a song
singing for all the ages

DO YOU STILL REMEMBER THE RIVER

Do you still remember the river?
how she turned and curved
covering our eyes with the leaves of young trees?
And later, without a word
we walked on for a long time
but never did discover where she began
in the end, we found only
a lovely little lamp
bathing quietly in the river

There're no flowers by the river now
only a path
as white as a thread
pulled from a ball of snow
and trees with black skin
fixed by the winter
magically in the snow
on the other side of the river, they too haven't forgotten
to find some fault with each other

The water flows on as before
when there is no one around
it sings its perplexing song
she comes from some place warm
so is not afraid of the flu
breathing out light puffs of air
the sky caught in the fork of the tree
is like a pane of frosted glass
on which she would paint a picture

I cannot paint, I really can't
I can only write notes in the snow
write down all that you want to know
come now, or you'll be late
before they melt away
pilfered by flowers that now understand these things
and handed over to fearsome bees
then, no honey
only the lamp standing there

THE WIND HAS STOLEN OUR PRIZE

And that's the way it was
                a gust of wind so gently
            stole our prize
the dark green water of the lake
sparkled playfully
                    "Let's go now, look no more
                    look no more for where it began"

With the excitement of the summer rain, perhaps,
                        the water-gates collapsed
        hidden in the tops of willow trees
a chorus of frogs
                    practices its songs
the autumn wind has, perhaps, blown dry the clouds
            so ants can bravely
        crawl out on the dry lotus leaves
                scanning the horizon from their tents

The row of old pilings perhaps
            still stands in the water

with the children waiting there for the minnows
the clean glass jar placed
upon the grass
perhaps the damp cicadas
like philosophic discourse
still crawl here and there
discarded coins
pondering the mud

think no more about it
think no more about where it began
the wind stole our prize
our
prize is on the bank of another springtime
the embankment long and narrow
the willow catkins have taken away the stars, only the
moon remains
only the moon remains
grazing our lips
illuminating that unknown road

FOR A LOST STAR

Why are you always watching me
all alone
not as beautiful as Cygnus
nor as plentiful as the Sisters
since the very beginning it has been so
no fault of your own

rather, the blame is mine
I've left so many people behind
or perhaps they've left me
I have no grinning flowers
no habit of distributing happy looks
I'm usually silent before the sages

Silent like a cloud at dusk
I do not know
do not know what you want, really I don't
entwining acacia trees conceal the sky

I'd guess, there will be many more nights like this
which is to say
I don't want you to be alone again

FOR MY GRANDMOTHER, NOW DEPARTED

In the end
I understand the failings of death
so short-lived
like a whistle
the chalk lines on the playing field already faded

Yesterday, in a dream
we were assigned our house again
you paced back and forth
scuffing your feet along the floor
dropping all your belongings
into the smallest corner

Just as before, you wash clothes late into the night
humming songs as old as
the wooden washtub
and you comb your white hair
with a broken comb
just as before, when you are happy
you open the satin, fold after fold
to show me
glass buttons now disappeared
but for a lifetime you have believed
they are as beautiful as diamonds

Just as before, I want to go out
to play or go to school
outside the arched screen door
on the fifth-floor landing
lighting the stove, lighting the stove
birds are all atwitter
the whole morning
floats in light blue smoke

My life revolves around you
just as yours revolves around me

DISTANT TRAVELER IN THE GRASSLANDS

You've trudged in from some place far away
and off you'll go again to some other place far away
toting along a common mission
a smile gleaming like black porcelain
and a heart as exhausted as dust
your luggage just keeps getting heavier all the time

But for now, you drop it all in the grass
surrounded by parades of toadstools, and patches of wildflowers
gazing up at you
as if you were some major holiday event
happily they crowd around, giggling
so much that some fear for their pretty uniforms

Of course, there are also companions like wild strawberries
who, with no concern for others, creep forward
grasping tightly with their tough, tentacled roots
raising their bodies up
perhaps they want to go deep into some desert
and listen to the sighs of the lifeless wind

Over blossoms and tossed hair
clouds, silver-gray, flecked with black ink float by
the sun erased by a light brush stroke
leaving behind only an elliptical patch of blue sky
so blue that it is like an ocean bay
or like the blue eyes of a young lover beside that bay

Together you gaze upward
you and the grasslands
forgetting the tremble of the hems and tattered leaves
forgetting how the lightning bolt sinks into the earth
only desire, in places near and far
glitters, your smiles so different

DUSK, WHO SAYS

Dusk, who says
dusk, with the sound of candy wrappers
friends here for the holidays
have come down off the mountain
the washed-gravel road
makes one think of the ocean's roar
down from the mountains, their young hands
each holding a bright red leaf
all behind the wings of dragonflies
clearly saying something
in the transparent and fragile air

Dusk, who says
dusk, with the sound of faraway digging
old apple trees
have nothing to say
the massive tumulus and flocks of mountains
slide together in the slanting light
the black elastic shadow
extended by time
fixed on the potter's wheel
no, there's no broken instance
there's no hero

Dusk, who says
dusk, with the sound of a glass scraped across the table
performing the world for a day
you should remove your make up
little by little washing away the fresh blood and pollen
there'll be no more tragedies, no more
audience, the last
little green girl, runs over, from some far place
runs over, jumps about, then stands still
waiting for her little brother
her smile like that of her mom

Bulin's File

1981–1982

ABOUT BULIN

When I was young, Bulin, a character sort of like Monkey King or Don Quixote, disturbed my thoughts. I was fascinated with how unruly he was and how he was always ready to skip school. Since he was always on my mind, I created stories about him, which I wrote down on pieces of paper. Sometimes I even used classical Chinese to write these stories, and accompanied them with illustrations.

Then, when I was twelve years old, we were sent to the countryside, and somehow I forgot all about Bulin. After that, I was busy trying to make a living and searching for the truth, and Bulin fell completely silent, as if he had died—perhaps he actually did die. Back then, if I looked over the things I had written when I was young, I found them amusing but not of any real interest.

The grind of time suppressed these things until one afternoon in June 1981, when I suddenly awoke. My dreams collapsed and I found Bulin everywhere around me, bringing with him a strange new world. My blood ran hot, and as my pen flew across the paper my hand was governed only by inspiration. It was as if I were on fire, as if I lived once again. I instantaneously abandoned all the lyric forms that I had struggled over for so long, and wrote five Bulin poems in one sitting. Later these would be extended to eighteen and form an experiment in fundamental self-renewal.[1]

After I had finished the "Bulin" sequence, I avoided it for a long time, even though a good number of my friends liked it. To me its introspection and lack of lyricism were too obvious and they bothered me. It was only after "Bulin" was published that I really began to see the poems for what they were, to see them through the eyes of a reader or critic. In its form, the sequence is like a modern fairy tale; its content is very realistic, but it is not a reality to which we are accustomed; it is the magic realism of Latin America. Nonetheless, it comes from this world of ours, not from some fantasy of desire.

---

1 Originally there were eighteen poems, but in 1992 the author eliminated two from the sequence.

1. The Birth and Emigration of Bulin

When Bulin was born
spiders were meeting
a dangerous dance, in the air
the music was terrible
and Bulin cried
slogans, slogans were all that he cried
poems of praise should not be so damn noisy
and then he smiled
a smile of perfect proportions
like a president up for reelection
thus, the mare there believed he had grown
and with one quick step he was out of his cradle
using a sheepskin
for his portfolio
he stuffed it with diapers of high confidences
and went off to work in the towers of government

No more dance parties
there
for the Strike Committee of Ministers
was holding an election
names covering cigarette papers
names written everywhere, and faces made
Bulin arrived
entering the meeting hall from the stable
as serious as a dark slab of marble
he stood still, with one finger raised
around which hung a brass horn
"Bread," he said,
the crows falling to the table, all cawing
"Yes, bread
is what we need, you understand,
for the pride of the people
Long Live Bread! **Don't add eggs,**
destroy the conspiracies of soufflé!"
all the people and trees
applauded
in order to heighten emotions
they also played distant recordings

and on the mouths of all the well-placed pigs
smiles were drawn in ink
unfortunately this is an art form
now lost to the past

When Bulin was done performing
lecture completed, he left the country as planned
in the twinkle of a star
he was at the harbor
it certainly couldn't have been easy
to trade rubber boots for a submarine
but everything went smoothly
and Bulin decended deep into international waters
where he ran into, not a whale, but rather
the crochet hook with which Santa Maria fished
and when Maria couldn't pull him up
she knew it was Bulin on the line
barefoot
she began to fly about the high seas
a crochet hook
dragging behind a submarine traded for boots
she flew here and there for two weeks
when suddenly Bulin surfaced for air
then again sank down in hunger
but Maria, of course, met with God early on
the race completed
two more centuries passed
before the hungry pleas began to lessen
two pairs of socks starved to death
a book of poems, and a brass screw

2. *Who Could Have Thought*

Who could have thought
that the dots of full stops would turn into peas
seeds sprouting deep in the night
piercing the stomachs of a hundred masterworks

Who could have thought
that Spain would turn into a harmonica
Lisbon

trembling like a brass reed
trembling its little tune
that brought blind musicians to the sea to panhandle their songs

Would could have thought
that Bulin would turn bad
concealing his toy pistol
together with several presidents, change professions
and seize the Bank of France

Who could have thought, but you should have known
that's why you need an imagination
to make poetry die of starvation
and turn it into a dog sniffing with its long snout
to make the enlarged legs of trousers
turn into sausages filled with beans

3. *Discoveries*

Of all the people who went to the snow-covered mountains
only Bulin found the road
although it was but a few meters long
and it was here that Venus
broke a tooth
even that did not deter
an Englishman from dying there
lying in the middle of the road smiling
out of his ear grew young leaves
and boughs of orchids
with a rosy complexion too

What did this all mean?
Bulin wondered, brow furled
in the end he remembered
when he was nine, it was here
that he spent the summer, planting matches in the ground
they sprouted and formed berries
the size of match heads
and in his greed
the Englishman ate them

This was the real discovery
unprecedented, perhaps—
          the fruit of matches are poisonous
Bulin began to make his way down the mountain
and stopped in front
of a Tibetan temple made of manure
he readied himself for someone, dagger in hand,
to rob him of this secret
but it never happened, and all he could do was
to sigh with all his heart
and bind up his socks with thin copper cables
and step out into the swamp

And there
his sandals scream excitedly
as they turn into a pond full of frogs

4. *Bulin Met a Bandit*

Bulin met a bandit
an actual bandit!

A descendent of the Horned Monster
in the stream, one hand on his beard
the other on his sword

He and Bulin
hacked and sliced, back and forth,
in the fissures of ochre-colored coal
slicing up alive eight hours and a wrist watch

Bulin was exhausted
and announced
the theater would hold an intermission
with that, the bandit seized
the fiberglass princess
wanting to steal her away

But, alas
fiberglass cannot be woven into a princess
better to weave a cover for a thermos

To run away?
but that takes some
special skill, most importantly
someone should be pursuing, and you cannot laugh

If you are not to laugh, then don't

Bulin and the princess
swam across the white porcelain washbasin
but couldn't climb up the full-length mirror

They're running for their lives,
but where is the person in pursuit now?
Bulin says he's exhausted
there needs to be an intermission

With fifteen cents
he stands in line to buy an ice-cream bar

5. Bulin's Entry for the Lullaby Competition

The blood of grapes fills the glass
and air fills the bronze bell
into the mouths of those who fancy death
are placed tear-gas bombs and a million words

Hey, **Little Treasure who no one wants**
Don't you cry, look,
there are angels of cream
hiding from the rain, under the arches of the bridge

As long as the torrent of mud holds off a little longer
they can finish their conference
a conference that decides to vacation inside your heart
where the rents are cheaper

6. Bulin's Speech to the National Conference of Nursery Schools

From the east, from the west, they come for money
from the north, from the south, they come for money

but money, I have none
if I did, I wouldn't give
if I gave, it wouldn't be much
if it weren't much, it would be of no use
because it would be counterfeit
because money, I have none

7. *The Original Recording of Bulin's Prayer*

Dear God, bless and protect our god
protect his family and his facial hair
bless his frequent performances on the road
and his wife's infrequent separations
protect the happy reunion of his many descendants
may they trample on but one ant in their park visit
bless and protect the subway built between his teeth
may it be able to bear the brunt of hydrogen bombs
and while You are at it, also bless and protect his daughters
may they be beautiful after their cosmetic surgery

Dear God, bless and protect our god
protect his coffee pot and his victory
let him eat more black tadpoles
but not life jackets or whales
protect the stalactites in his left ear
that it may become a scenic spot
let him be punctual and in perfect measure
as he converts his followers into electric toys
and while You are at it, also bless his favorite breakfast
sun and tomato side by side on a plate

Dear God, bless and protect our god
protect his paycheck and his reputation
bless him with words of flexibility
such that he is able to make a couch or a recliner
bless his ever-expanding soap bubbles
save them from shattering the air when they burst
of the many caterpillars he captures
let them be fashioned into clothes made of tiger pelts
and finally, take a little more time to bless the Blessing Agency
so that they won't declare bankruptcy

Yes, God, our Lord, bless and protect our god
protect him as You would protect Yourself
and the self, what sort of thing is that?
who's to know, perhaps it is a
metal pail that does not sound when struck, or an instrument of transport
in any event, bless and protect all these things, and if the sky darkens
so blessings aren't given, it does not matter
I cannot in fact proclaim "Amen"
for "Amen," like fresh chili powder
easily gives one unexpectedly explosive breath

8. Bulin's Military March

One hundred and eight thousand miles
away from the very first words
we'd like to eat popsicles
but are seated at some banquet

Butter-knife in hand, off to the front of the line
toting a water bottle, I search for you
along the English coastline
cast in yellow and green
on the map

The stairs are drawn
the guests may return
one hundred and eight thousand miles
away from the very first words

9. Bulin's Military Anti-March

Dreaming of a tree
with branches piled high
a kid
splashes in the mud
and a hundred kids
stand by celebrating his birthday
all leave
with cake in hand
two people memorizing faces

three people forgetting them
cars block the intersection
so there's never any leaving

10. *Proposal Number 0*

Everyone with long golden fingernails
should have them cut
because Bulin is out of work
the newly sprouted moon is thin and curved
because bars of gold and blocks of ice
are about to be wed
every home needs a combination lock
every purse, a zipper
because danger is born
the crab and round brown cupcake crawl
out of the film studio
down to the beach

11. *Research*

How did B. B. die?
he left Bulin so angry
Bulin
took
the prize

Why did Bulin take the prize?
he was so angry at B. B.
B. B.
left the prize
behind

12. *Couplet*

The smokestack is a chimney that the chimney doesn't recognize
the chimney is a smokestack that the smokestack doesn't recognize

The long-snouted beetle flicks itself into the sky

13. *It Would Seem Bulin Is Dead*

Curses and large frogs
fall, tripped, onto the wall
it would seem
Bulin is dead
in the end, God politely took out his handkerchief
and in the cemetery
a bed of square blossoms
popped open

Alas, it would seem, Bulin is dead
his hundred grimy-faced grandsons
come in red cars from the heart
of the continent, hurrying to mourn him
weeping briefly with high-pressure hoses
filing their teeth, they then begin to
disco
spreading wide their stubby fingers
opening their mouths, there appear billiard balls
half an ice-cream sun
a refrigerator
bubbles of dark beer floating in the air

Uh-oh
Bulin is dead, dead, dead
a death so well practiced, as if it were real
he blinks inside the heating pipes
regretting
he brought so few
sleeping pills

14. *Funeral Dirge*

A potato on a moonlit night
a potato on a moonlit night

And along comes a dog
to sniff
a potato on a moonlit night

15. A News Item

A dog
was executed by America
because it had a pair of girls
in its wallet

The girls were always together
talking about collars and curtains
talking about how the teacher after gym class
wore a shirt of coarse linen

16. Bulin's Last Instructions

All those who come to trade in tragedy
must stick together
like cabbage leaves
and find that one and only way
to turn the pyramid around
so the four sides soak in the sunlight

Wind Dreams

1982

I'LL BE GOING NOW

Taking leave of the clock tower on its night watch
thank you, I'll be going now
and I'll take with me all my stars
so I never again have to fret their loss

Taking leave of the heavy fence
yes, I'll be going now
please don't tell the crows in the temple
the story that you have heard about stealing apples

At last, taking leave of the fine sand on the river bank
good night, I'll be going now
no one here has yet gone off to that eternal sleep
waiting for the cross to grow roots and bear its fruit

I'll be going now, going
off toward the far edge of that green and misty sky
I am gone. But how is it that I have come to your window again
and from its edge flutters the handkerchief's signal of our meeting

It's not my mistake, no
it is that dumb, dusty pony
who didn't understand last night's awful promise
it is he who has brought me back to you again

ONE SPRING DAY

Outside the wood-framed window
lie my cultivated fields
my little yak
and my single-bladed plow

A troop of sunshine soldiers
works its way through the fence
and the sky-blue flowers
begin to bend their petals there

The dew's fears
soak into the slice of memory
frightened grosbeaks
jump here and there

I want to go to work
to select seeds from within a dream
letting them gleam in the palm of my hand
and then fall, all into the water

WIND DREAMS

It's winter
and from the large porcelain vase
the wind moans on forever
then later, so tired
it thinks no one has heard
there's no road through to the south
or to the city where white birds roost
and where the granite is fond of dew

It falls off to sleep, turning and tossing
like those strange willows that are always asking for understanding
like those hibernating snakes
under the tree

It begins to dream
dreaming its own aspirations
just like stars, sparks from the flint
it dreams in the instant of the strike
it struggles forth, turning into flame
and it hopes that those pallid hands
will be able to expand
becoming soft and intimate
not to be severed
by a splinter of the shattered moon

Later, it dreams again
of a small village
like a large wooden boat rocking stubbornly
in the northern night
countless dark-colored ripples
are just now spreading
in the place nearing dawn
becoming a patch of light-blue foam

Because of the unfamiliar light
the frightened dog barks
for its master
because of those senseless fears and needs
it barks and barks
beside the earthen wall
and something falls into the pile of straw

Finally it dreams
that it's always waking
a small saltwater fish burrows into the mud
particles of wet sand clumped
like a strange pile of tan stones
in a place not far away
the waves sigh on
in the end, moving along that small lovely spine
and surging up to the sky

In the soaking sunlight
there is no dust
the shells continue to squint

Spring, spring has come
so near
while others pay no attention
it changes into its dark-purple dress

Yes, it awakes
awakes into a shining dream
gazing intently on the sky, face washed and hair combed
it grows
according to its own hopes, grows in youthful ways
legs so long and slim
slightly parted
in a faraway place
rocking this piece of land

BUDDHA WORDS

I am poor
with no place to go cry in pain

My profession is fixed
fixed to sit here
sit for a thousand years
to practice the richest of smiles
and still I'll hold out my hand delicately
as if I were giving something to mankind

I've no idea what to give
and no desire to get
I can only hope to preserve my tears
preserving them until my work is done

The dark green sandalwood is withered and gone
the dry red stars
have all fallen from the sky

A BANNER

Death is a relatively minor procedure
just a small excision of life
it doesn't even leave a scar

And after the procedure the patient is remarkably calm

ON THE LEFT-HAND SIDE OF THE DARK NIGHT

On the left-hand side of the dark night
a silvery fish
with its belly torn open
entrails gone
just one sticky eye remains
that eye fixed on me

It says
swimming below in the deep blue pool
with currents rapid and strong

the rock drill obeys its own magic
always dancing along the ledge
it says
stones resolute and strong
are all my brothers

SUMMER OUTSIDE THE WINDOW

Through the deep night a voice cries on and on
when the sun rises
the drops of rain sparkle briefly
then transform into steam
but I do not go to wipe off the glass
I know that the sky is blue
and every tree raises its hair in its hands
in that sound of snapping castanets
would be a big black beetle in search of food

Everything is so distant

I was once as weak as a morning cicada
wings soaked through
and leaves thick, we were young
knew nothing
and didn't want to know
all we knew was that the dreams might float up
might carry us into the daylight
clouds might walk along the wind
and the water of the lake might gather the light into flames

We look out at leaves turning green

Still I don't want to know
and have not got up to wipe off the glass
dark green waves of summer rise and fall
oars knocking, knocking
fish parting the glossy current
the smile of the red bathing suit slowly vanishing
everything is so distant
and still the summer procrastinates
and now the whispers end

SEPARATING

The black ooze seeps up from the mountain gorge
crows can fly
and take away my wings

Still I will stay here in this world
among the thin, dying grasses
my heart in the end always wanting to roll down
and transform into a stone

I know history
and that roly-poly business man
purchasing wings to sell
he and his bag both trembling
walking down the mountain
sighing his usual sighs

AGAINST THE CURRENT

I've gotten used to your beauty now
just as you've gotten used to mine
in the fading light we
sigh a sigh
and then shine upon each other

In the deepest part of the sea
we dare to breathe
breathing very slowly
feet dangling in shallows
not yet turned to fish

They cannot swim away
breathing in winter too
whoever pushes open the window
will see
the sea change into a puddle

In the north there's a summer palace
that you can reach across a bridge
you can kiss the snow newly fallen

on the ice flow
and afterward lean tight against the wall

That warm, warm wall
a wall of
desert, fire, and sun
I don't really believe
that it was you

I don't really believe
that she was you
so many years ago
near those glittering rocks
she was you

She stood below so low
the sky shining between her brows
colored rain now falling gently down
with praises made to god

FROM A BIRD'S-EYE VIEW TO THE WATERLINE

The smooth, rolling, coffee-colored currents of air
let me see into the silence
let me see the gravel
spewing forth into the midday sun
performing for us
off to infiltrate some delicate divinities
I see horsemen there
stripped of their leather clothes
hair and beards streaming in the wind
they turn their backs
and tumble, two by two, into the boulders
no one dares move
no fingers
dare mutate into the backbones of fish

And yet
the curve of the embrace is forever
it will never sink away

bent there for love
to protect the clear, cloudless sky
within the rock strata
an oval patch of clear
blue sky
like a small cameo in enamel
and there's also the sea
and the water-logged boat too
that swings on the waves of this small infinity
and there's salt
grain upon grain of saline glitter

I'm there
hauling weeds out from the sea
but it will not help
the ocean breathe
each opening in the net festering with infection
sent off by waves
covered with gentle mounds of green
I shiver a little
the water is hot in the sun
my skin turning red
at the end of the well-arranged wall of stone
hangs the flag of a shadow
the water line rises and falls
rolling this way and that

THE ART OF PULLING STRINGS

1.

Children trap bees
for their flowers
the world traps people
for itself
threading the lightning rod
he winds the string around his palm
and uses his other hand
to apply moon paste to his face
and, afterward sinking slightly down,
pulls the curtain up

2.

As the day grows light
all the people begin
to wave their hands and stamp their feet
they grab hold of buoyant leather bags
frantically
surging from the east side of town to the west
they step over the railroad tracks
no grass grows along the rails
stones are stuck in the tar
like a sesame toffee

3.

The string, a fishing line
caught there by sunlight in water
all our desires
can be drawn out into transparent silk
one only needs seduction
performed under water
isn't it amazing
how jumping in despair
the fish in the end learns
the proper application of fish bones

4.

Hanging high in that empty sky
first light, then heavy, a shining thread
man grows tall in the whirring sounds
the crane tower salutes in some nation's style
pay it no mind
just remember
those flowers there
and that bee
the Loch Ness monster awakes in the lake
and wild rabbits dash across the fields

THE COOLEST OF MORNINGS

A tree turns its back to cry
it starts with one tree
but later it's the whole tribe
they cry until dawn's light
a snow-like dust covering all this

All this floating in the dust
in the slightly interlocking shadows
with footsteps, suddenly light then dark
hunters, walking a straight line,
keep retracing their steps from the border

In the heart of the early morning
there's just one cuddly cub
pampering itself
as if it were
the only daughter of the snowy mountains

ORIENTAL COURTYARD

It is loneliness
that has turned me into an old man
wiping away the rust from the radio broadcast
with brick ash
I move nearer to the courtyard wall
to dig out roots from the wet ground
a transparent tune keeps surging forth

In the kindergarten on the other side of the wall
children clap their hands
sunlight sparkles there for only an instant
the water of the lake is green
dark shadows retreat into a kiss
in the grass, large drops of dew
and also some fallen leaves

I like that tree there
his patterned hands
and dull-witted ways

footsteps come to a stop
faraway on the freshly washed steps
grapevines and iron railings
invent new feelings

In the grass there are also
silver spider webs
and cicadas like marionettes
crawling toward the tree
and those toads too
moving their bellies along
wanting to be better at jumping

Everything wants to be better at something
including the autumn
taking off his wet clothes
and drying them out there
including towns of the American West
and tough guys, tough guys
talking with gear-wheel jaws

I'm an old man now
all is at peace in the oriental courtyard
life and clouds in one place
birds sing winding melodies
sunlight moves through the dew
it is love that
moves me nearer to the clear blue sky

THE OLD ONE

Beyond the glass
someone says, "She's fallen ill."
and I think of you

The hallway begins someplace faraway
and then turns again
you are on the north side

Every day on the north side
twenty years now

beyond the door, another door, a room and a balcony
beyond the window, another window and a balcony
it's a long way down
to the ground, they say

The window forever faces north
in the dazzling noon light, all is the same
the south side, empty
sunlight like syrup left out to cool

The window forever faces north
looking out from the head of the bed
your careful gaze finally falls upon something there
don't worry now
the pigeons will be out on the roof again

The door moves a bit
but there's no one there
a line of light falls below the door, then no more
to the north it's clear and pale
like plain hot water with no tea
no one talks to you

Your daughter died, long ago
somewhere on the road
and that is her red case there, and her clock too
her daughter has now grown
and works to care for a daughter of her own

Today it's really windy
so go ahead and remember her
the thread lies in pieces
and can't be threaded anymore, but still there're things to be mended
the shadows are always there, outside the window
always as still and flat as glass

There used to be a copper kettle
old, placed over the flames
dried branches rubbing against each other
singing, they returned light to the sun
each and every pouring
making dust rise up in clouds

How wonderful
warm death
dangerous steps
everyone falls in love once
waking up is not all that strange

BETWEEN WAITING AND ARRIVAL

Year after year you
spin your revolver round
a life between waiting and arrival
hammer pulled back
steel hesitating before the strike
the light in the water wriggling like a worm

You spin it one more time
the rim of the muzzle thinned
the color of brass, slightly upward opening
who crushed the cinders?
monkey rubbing its thick lips
unable to put its voice in good order

When you sleep you put it under your pillow
put it under the fault line
like a rodent getting out of the wind
bullets hide in their burrows
each one, moist
like tiny seeds of musk

All eyes seen by guns
are blackened
black waiting for day
morning cocooned in the treetops
a sun, a sun flying away
with an explosion

You're forever spinning your revolver round
standing on the edge of the bank
your hand in the current of the river
turning round the water wheel of the South
pestle slowly rising up and falling down
so slowly there is no way for the song to begin

I Dreamt of Fishes

1983

THE GROUND

I touch you lightly
dry mane, thick and stiff
fat badgers, so many like this
sleeping
tightly wound   with their snouts
pushed against their burrows   stifling
a yawn, dark red and reeking
filled with dreams
that are piled up like old bricks   no way of knowing
the suffering of the honeybee

I belong with you lightly too
my hopes
are not dull   a small knife
drawn back and forth across the leather strap
dangerous rainbow
dangerous smile of the sea
there's no one   in the morning
in front of the window of blue sky
curled up there
the shape of a bear

I DREAMT OF FISHES

I dreamt of fishes
in the dark green night

They moved lightly by
pressing close to me
small sails raised on their bronze backs

They drank things in
with velvet mouths
as if they were curved knives guarding the dark
there were footsteps on the staircase
then after a while
gills opening
blood red, red
like a wound opened wide
water fleas jumping hard and high
and then slowly sinking down
timed to the rhythm of a waltz

Their eyes opened wide all the time
slipping through the ranks of surreal railings
to keep their tears from falling

Without moving a muscle
they go forward
the stars of Andromeda glitter in succession

INTO A STILL LIFE

It's springtime on that grassy slope
disheveled hair now neatly rearranged
the scarlet hairband tightened round
a fat white cat represents the sun
head turned, looking
in constant contemplation of the mad dash
the reflecting light in diamond shapes
the window always open
the curtain hanging
always hiding away from the wind's approach

Inside the room, a bird of red wood
and a bronze drum beaten
it is getting late
fifty thousand years ago
the river's current cut through
the loose soil of the plateau
and humans walked down the river valley

searching for something in the icy water
picking up a round stone
to grind the morning's food

Bread, still life's most beautiful object
there is always bread, fresh
breath filled with light
light brighter than a dinner knife
making one think of Germany
and there's something more
one cup, and another
on the flat white tablecloth
and several pieces of freshly peeled fruit
all one could ever hope for

WELDED HEAT

1.

Blood filled with foam and bubbles
sunlight moves along beside me
                    stones tumble down
                    tumble down for so long
one by one abandoning their iron jug
the spring rain is green
summer streams sing through the deep valleys
there are trees here
the maiden of the Lone Dragons wants to turn away
and observe flocks of birds through her falling hair

The dripping sounds
keep coming, coming

2.

Again it seems so long ago

Barefoot, you
lit up the shark's spinal curve
again it seems so long ago

that fin spread wide, now dry
and dry too their black and white spikes
all through the dusk comes a putrid light

Barefoot, you
wait for the wind to blow across the dunes
wait for the wind to blow across the soon-collapsing dunes
dusk seeps through the putrid light
miles of salt solidified
iron rods test their depths
miles of salt soaking wet
the sea sparkles far away
a sea of squirming, silver hairpins
sparkles far away
the deep blue enamel sea

3.

The lamp, moving ever so slightly
descends
I do not know why we need tiles
or need the pure red flames
or tiles that reflect the light
why do you need to go touch them
there in that ever-darkening kiln

Paper flames
the shadow of someone burns in paper

Along the edges
sparks of starlight refuse to die
bubbles of starlight's sparks
refuse to die
insects of starlight
transparent pillars of smoke
insects of starlight
my warm and pleasant melancholy reaches its peak

POVERTY, IT HAS AS A COLD WET NOSE

Poverty, it has a cold wet nose
speaking through a crystal ball
after water drops have died of thirst

On every side stand fields of wheat
all is cast in the sun's golden glare
all is dust blown in by its hot breath
the stems twisted
hot and scorched
women in pink walk along the dike
field mice fall through the open door
fall into ashes
a colorless flame burns on the stove

Poverty, it has a cold wet nose

A WIND BLOWS THROUGH THE BUILDINGS

A wind blows through the buildings
a chilly wet wind
I won't miss this city then
its leaves enormously turning
fallen leaves plugging the drains
I don't want to know
green iron on the door
copper on the window
green iron on the window
copper on the door
I don't want to know
the soggy flowers falling, falling

In a place far far away
on a night even cooler still
you walk along the levee
the ocean keeps your melancholy company
you walk the long embankment
to the far ends that are over there

THIS DEEP DARK DITCH

From this deep dark ditch
someone with graying hair
lifts a bucket
diamonds of water's light
a ditch at the edge of the woods

Bottles bob to the surface
and with them windows rise and fall
rust-colored dust lies on the window ledge
the guts of dusky fish
spill out

Unlocking locks in the air
bronze shells, thin as gills
a lamp shines on
the wooden treads of the stairs
the old books writing their old poems

Before dinner you are always waiting for someone
disciple on the balcony
a door handle
with moonlight opening the sky
inside the room, a round table, all set and ready

CONFESSION

I must confess
I watch you washing the dinner glasses
washing with your fingers so very long
the water rubbing strangely inside the glass

From there you walk over here
where are your clothes?
I can't see the glass
only the roundness of the water moving back and forth

Yes, there is a world
a mirror where we can enter
from here you walk over there
a lifetime of avoiding me

A VILLAGE WITH NO ONE IN IT

A village with no one in it
walls of granulated sugar
and a small canal flowing toward the shade
dried leaves dream on
inside the fence, piles of leaves
walls of granulated sugar
and behind, sunflowers are black
walls of granulated sugar
sawflies ruin the view
a village with no one in it
tree limbs begin to move two by two
softly treading on the stairs
aardvarks crouch all around

ALL THOSE STORIES

A.

I float up from water's depths
the way of grape-stealing shards

B.

Many people stand at the station
investigating umbrellas

C.

The words are all stuffed into a small cup
the peelings of fruit

D.

Behind the empty, swaying railway cars
blue sky, you disappeared

E.

Those beautiful heads
with their smudged eyebrows raised

F.

You are far away
you tell my heart to keep on walking

G.

On the bank
weeping after the boulders have tumbled down

H.

Waves of the ocean, gray in May
the swallows call your name

SITTING HERE ON HEAVEN'S STEPS

Sitting here on Heaven's steps
I really would like something salty

And what would you like, God
and what is your nationality?
with your sky-blue beard
you would like to be in a vaudeville
I wrote a poem
for which I am guilty
so here I sit
have a seat, don't worry about your pants

Down below, life still goes on
go and look, there at the railing
springtime is crossing the road
crossing the road with a flock of yellow primrose in tow
it has rained just now
the woods are damp and moldy
there are mushrooms, and there are rooms of nuns

ALL'S FINE

"All's fine"
I don't know what else could still burn
in this dark and silent night
there's still dripping rain and fresh blood
that bring a smile
along that dark gray street in fits and starts we proceed
meticulously sorted by type
and inserted into bins that are opened daily
gray clouds accompany us on our way to work

We look down at fur standing stiffly on our paws

We had turned into a pack of wolves among the stones
then into sheep
sparkling, we walk on in fits and starts
tears don't allow a howl
our shadows never say, "It's fine"
shadows point their mouths toward the road
they let us know, stalks of wheat are in the bins
stalks of wheat are in the bins, stalks of wheat are in the bins

WORK

Tears have soaked through so many days
but today the sky is blue and doves are on the wall
my bed goes back inside again
renewed hopes, this small patch of clear sky
today is a fine and sunny day
I ought to be writing poems of joy
but I need to cut away one more small square
and slowly retreat
I need two rows of youthful teeth
rain flows out from the wall again
I push aside the world, and slowly retreat
morning enlarges the entire square
behind it, a muddy street slants away
white clothes are like small dots
behind the wall people ask
Is this that world?

WALLED DREAMS, AND AN AWAKENING

1.

I wait forever
for the wall
to awake

Leaves have fallen to the ground
leaving behind nothing but a bird and its nest
quiet on my birthday

Withered grass on all sides
parched but still alive

In the narrow lane crickets research their music
my birthday comes in the fall

I can only speak of
the many stones cast down
by the sun, a sign of the living

2.

I began this wait
many years ago

Snowflakes scattered across the concrete
ice on the pond
smooth and glittering in the dark night
and logs trapped in the water

The atmospheric blue will crush this room
I'd like to turn and walk away

I stare out from this pristine life

Sparrows beat their wings against the barn door
the stone mill stands among the yams
the air dark, dank, and cool

I look out from this small window with its smooth eyelids
sleepy panes of paper

3.

Because of the stars
the rains continue to seep through the roof

Gray tiles pressing down together
a dim-witted crow
there's no omen whatsoever

The books slide down
slide down onto my shoulders, my hands a little numb
the bird of my voice
has no companion

A fire burns on the dark water
fire of beauty
a fragrant beauty
the water's sweet smile meets the wall

My breathing
is a paper boat

4.

Have you heard about the canyons?
the many canyons of the world
and in some there are temples and branches of trees

But the canyon of which I speak is even farther away
even farther away water remains in the night

I've rubbed the stones, stones warm
released by the sun
stones not carried away by the water

Dusk in the canyon
is a flame diluted by shades of green
I long for that dusk

The wall, the wall smiles within the stones

The small boat strikes against the wall

it rubs against it with a hand of lamplight
that lamp is my gift

5.

Silently the wall tries on its clothes

Ashes on the shallow water
welcoming something, or running away
I fear the dark night deep beneath the waves

Born unfit to be a fish
but I still have fish temptations

The boat still rubs along the surface of the water
on the water, a cavern drinking in the wind
you want to run away, but still the many criteria remain

The water offers its full lips
pressing close to the bank, one kiss after another
in windows of a well-lit house on the bank
hang burning tinder

A boat of steel draws near

6.

I need to get up and move about
my hands want to see the spring
the springtime of cigarette wrappers

The wall of dawn follows me
helmeted dawn

Over the high plateau hang clods of dirt
clods hang from my shoulders
my heart is a clod

The giant floor of dawn comes twisting and turning
forcing me to think of fish in the kitchen smoke
fish have no branching tendrils
but birds seem to
floating in the light

The little bellows forever sucking in the wind

Watching the sun
largely watching the sun without mist
I live in the surface of shadows.

7.

I've almost seen the spring
that my hands have seen, covered with pollen
she can't deceive me now

Then have you gone off to the graveyard?

The wall is single-sided
like a sheet of paper with writing on one side only

I'm no bird
my voice has not gone there

A place without water
and without canyons either
emulsion-colored bubbles collapse
one place of hunger
one place of thirst
half-moon bellies all in a row

Humanity perfectly packaged

I wish there were a wall

8.

In the end the earth stands erect
just as I walk atop the wall
this is now my only road

That is now my only road

Galaxies of light swim toward me
threads of tiny algae-eating fish

almost laughing
my hand opens wide like a net
do I have no net?

The moon has its shell

And flames drip quickly down through the cracks
honeyed drops of transparent flame
blacken my ears with soot

9.

Yesterday we lost our electricity
the moon was our only lamp

The armpit of the city piled with hot burning coal
troops on the road
You slept in the bed
your feet planted there on the wall
your toes are growing into the wall

You went and closed the window tight
calling the raindrops fish
rain on the piles of copper
small stagnant pools of water

I would like a wall that can walk about
a wall that can walk about
that can walk about

Over there, a shoji screen

10.

Doors made of glass
sparkling glass turning round and round

Broad leaves begin to glisten now
in this morning of sorts
veins fill the leafy hearts
and the sun starts its invasion

When the conference opens
the earth rattles its spears
putting up light resistance

This is a morning of "one"
the sugar-cube city is everywhere

Iron railings stand meekly on four sides
undulating shadows fill the center
outside, grass that no longer breathes

Reach out with your hand, slowly, please

MANTIS ROMANCE—A FABLE

The large female mantis
marches slowly through the tangled weeds
and there happens upon
her husband, pathetic
with wings as thin
as dried bamboo leaves
and big green eyes like
drops of tears

With her delicate antennae
she caresses his sorrowful brow
he raises his two legs
as if praying for help
and they make love
in the late fall afternoon
grass and trees rattle in the breeze
the sun moves into the valley

The wind cools
dusk begins to fill the sky
the female mantis shakes out her thin blouse
and tightens the sash around her fat little belly
she turns to her husband then
as if to give him one last kiss
swiftly bites off
his head

The last rays of light still bright
shine on this lovely world
fall upon broken wings in the weeds
wings that still want to dance in flight
this is the romance of mantis
forever together, until the end
not like people here
with all our sordid affairs

STREWN

Where the highway turns to byway
there the grass turns to woods

My heart is filled with desolation
a puddle forms under my tongue

Shadows seep out from my body
I come from within the lamp

I slide crabgrass into the window
eyes behind, hands out on the street

Eulogy to the World

1983–1985

ABOUT "EULOGY TO THE WORLD"

. . . For two years, I have been rereading myself, the passions of the past trans-
formed into tangible things—beliefs, pen-stands, talents all mixed together. In
the end they cast a small glimmer of light; I watched with wonder as my hand
moves along the branch, moving to the left, taking hold of a leaf.

—January 1986

1. The Ability of the Tree to Swim

The ability of the tree to swim
is what keeps the birds on course
recalling the sound of lake waters
the birds sing in flight
      noon, they say
        the age of treetops, they say

Fragrance covers our bodies
long cool arms pass through our hearts
we swim through the wind
formed in silence and solitude
we cannot see our very first day
at first, when there was only love

2. A Prompt

Married to a girl
living inside the body of a lute
you listen to the wind blow with the music of her heart
you watch her walk away from the bed, toward the window
the sea softly rolls

boulders lie there still
John is your name
Ann is your road

3. *Youth*

The earth crashes gently down

The moon rises up

Ripples of water in the iron kettle

4. *Growing Up*

Everyone stares at me
all those fingers of flame
I avoid the sunlight, walking through the ranks of cypress trees
I turn away from feminine summer
green tiles on the red lawn
men covered with hair like banyan groves
I go off to eat at the dining hall
where wooden chopsticks gently click
through the garden opposite
walk children with an element of gold

5. *Ark*

You've boarded a giant ship that will surely sink
and disappear into the ocean's heavy breathing
but there you are still watching the flag
and that grassland as it darkly spreads
seabirds call out from the graveyard of the waves
but you still amuse yourself at the railing
amazed by the sound of deck chairs sliding away
with no one in them, and all the doors opened
waiting for the cold flames to rise from sailors' cabins

6. A Request for a Painting

Over the expanse, expanse of newly plowed land, that expanse, expanse of
    land already plowed, the air turns fresh and clean
a pale blue sky the color of fish, crows cast over the ground, crows that
    cannot fly
a warrior in green rubber boots, climbs the river bank, searching for a youth
a boy twelve years old, traveling from the capital to the provinces, a world
    like a wheel fallen from its axle
there he has a small place, far far from the village, where the world circles
    round
in the heavy mud, the thick and heavy mud, he meets the green-booted
    warrior
inside his horsehide armor, a pen and a sheet of light gray paper
he asks him to draw the imperial city, the temple for the gods, lions and
    bells of bronze
to draw ice cream, radio towers, zebras and envoys wandering near the
    observatory
South Americans, North Americans, Hawaiians, and red sleet slanting
    through the air
paper spread out on the hot stove, winter burns inside, the boy hasn't
    studied art
he's drawn horned monsters, eyes on Buddhist pedestals, but never palace
    banners
he's written explanations on wings of ambulances, a few lines blank, while
    mountain yams cook in the pot
the silver light of steam fills the doorway, the imperial city complete on the
    stove, included are telephones from nations around the world
the warrior thanks the boy, presents him with a knife of stainless steel, ciga-
    rettes and snake teeth
outside, land of the yellow race, sun frightening in its blaze, the drawing
    slowly rolled up
skeletons lie in the ground of clay, knives in their hands, sinking obliquely
    into the sea
on the riverbank the warrior leaves, and then the boy leaves, crows spat-
    tered like ink along a beach

7. Inside the Bottle

Through the tiny glass mouth
of the life in which we reside
we can see the world above

Crows plunge straight into the sea
we can see roses and the seedy heads of cattails

We'll never reach the roses
nor touch the soft green threads of earth

8. *"Movements"*

"Movements," in the end, emerge from thin air
        the memories of summer reeds
        after August
"movements" are the shriveled corpses
        caught in the metal screen
        words written by a baby
"movements" are lizards suddenly appearing
        in the crowd at the vegetable stand
        crawling up the wall on all fours
"movements" are soldiers with smashed skulls
        either one by itself, or many
"movements" are roads delineated
                            by the hands of fantasy
"movements" are hopeless marriages
        unending downpours
        immovable concrete structures
"movements" have voices that grow ever lower
"movements" are faces spread out
        on winter's wall

9. *A Dark Television*

Two kids damming up a brook
tree branches stuck deep into the water

Two kids damming up a brook
tree branches stuck deep into the water

In the trees, the tongues of sound move in and out

Two kids walk across their dam

10. I Gather Together Golden Threads of Smoke

Still I gather together golden threads of smoke
"No," you say, taking hold of my hand,
the vein in your still arm moving toward its peak
recently you have been lifted up and sent to your grave
there you now push aside white stones and bouquets

"No," you say, with golden eyebrows coated, it seems, with cooking smoke
you tell stories about the afternoon after the peace has come
villages on green riverbanks with sparkling waters
a thicket filled with peacock pride
a bather, hornets crawling all over his wilting clothes

Their pencils worn down with sharpening, students stand on the bridge spitting
with poplar branches they attack each other
after a while, a wine merchant and his small brown pony come by
a pair of red-cheeked mothers toting children and coconuts
stop for the longest time, then there comes a soldier of shiny borders

A wire is snagged some place in the lower reaches of the river
where a hand rises from the water, history lying quietly on the grassy plains
the river weeps and kisses him on the lips
river fog sinks into the valley, red birds peck for food among the roots
and you say again, "The air, the air is so clean and cool"

11. Uprising

The water is covered with floating coins
the horns of the ox curve unexpectedly

12. Cars

The person you are to read
is getting dressed

You shine the reflected light into the back bedroom

There you sink together into the surface of the mirror

13. *The Source*

Along the staircase of the stream
horses from the forest walk on its metal chain

My flowers all come from dreams

My flames
the blue of the sea
best troops of the wide-open air

My dreams all come from water

Link by link in sunlight's chain
air from the wooden box
with the bearing of fish or birds

In a low voice I call your name

14. *Words*

We were almost crushed by the huge metal door
short little feet tromping in the sand
short little feet in indescribable pain

Out behind Abinn[1]

15. *A Narrative*

Three men ran away from the battlefield

They stirred leaves into their drinks, and gave their bullets away in the
    night
walking through the floating silk of market towns

And later, there came the MPs

He was the last one dragged through the public square

---

1 Abinn is a proper name, but it is not clear what the reference is.

16. One's Self

A face stroked by the cruel wind
a face only vaguely loved

It's been a long time now
a face holding tight to firewood like a brother

A face as coarse as rope
can only tightly love
can only be woven into a fence, or basket
to love her winter kindling

It's been a long time now
till the very end she does not, with her hand held out
touch the flower on her head

17. In That Little Village

In that little village
there's someone
dressed like a gingko tree

That's me, with eyes clouded by the morning
sand, white and gleaming
even the flecks of flies are undamaged

Transparent mountains rise and fall all around
wind like water in a brook
and the lakes of your eyes are clear of weeds

The unpainted village
gazes out at the sun from beneath the deep green water
we're fond of these villages of the sun

Living inside your love
breathing only once in a long while
streams glitter in the distant wasteland

Leaves fly and dance through the village

we have an open piece of land
and won't ask what the future holds

18. *Accessory to a Crime*

You're forever looking at the world out there
while your feet search for their slippers
you were married
and had some dark land for wheat
you stole things in your dreams

Once again you look at the staircase out there

19. *Middle of the Month*

Toppling over, sticking to the surface of the water
I think of my hands as pigeons
my shadow as a cavern
in daylight fat little birds peck for food at the mouth of my cave

The water jar gently weeps

20. *Up Early*

The water for boiling corn should be clean
pushed against the wall with rays of light

With a drop of water
tipping the shadow slowly into the fog

The place where the coffin lies is wet

The first god was of wax

The first riddle was oneself

The wooden door groans open, a deep blue sky
I approach in all seriousness

21. *Misfortune that Arrives at Its Appointed Time*

Misfortune that arrives at its appointed time
yet still does not beat down
the one speaking in front of the troops of tragedy

Their banners drag across their feet
layers of dream-shadows lie over their eyes
the herds of elephants go off to worship

The violence of
clothes, tongues and fresh flowers

Until the very end people weep without courage
reaching out from the open land toward the trees along the beach

22. *After the Air Raid Had Passed*

After the air raid had passed
we began to speak of poetry again
the ground soaking wet
everywhere lay shattered pottery

Just then you walked in
carrying a basket weighty
with food that you brought for me
bread and golden honey

Just two weeks after your death
I too died there in battle
emerald green grasses
now sealing up this trench

23. *Mouth of the River*

Someone who will be neither pigeon nor flower lies on his back gazing up
those dreams of dirt piles
those villages wanted in the dream
on the hillside someone plants burdocks, on the wall someone
spreads water, he lies there now, not wanting to get up

He knows the shadows of flowers, the shadows of starfish
he knows that shadows are the sea
　　　　the lush parade moves upward, offering praise

There always will be someone to become ashes of the grasslands
to become snow melting out of villages, crows wilting
　　　　weighty birds turning the soil over in the fields

There always will be someone to become the walkway for the blind, and
　　　for songs
there always is a hand reaching toward the land of the soul

There always will be someone thinking, cool flashes of light crossing his
　　　face

There always will be trees that separate the air and water, that separate
　　　earth
to bring to an end life's breathing, wrapped in its own fragrance

24. The Four Seasons: Preserving Dusk and Dawn

1.

For so many years, till the very end
I've lived in the valley of your breathing
I have built myself a house there
fixed the fence, and fallen asleep listening to the murmur of the brook,
　　　transparent claws among purple blossoms
I feel time
swirling meekly
up to the top of my head

The sun is as sleepy as a lion
the sun is as sleepy as a lion

So many shadows of bat-wing blossoms

Those cliffs that appear only at dusk

Words the cliffs repeat to me
words the streams repeat to me
white books and dense thickets

2.

Every day I drink water from that stream
with a copper flask I have
I know that the East is limitless, then
So must be the West, little by little the sea
bleeds into the mouth of my river, the lake shore
is hundreds of miles of white dunes

Eagles above the desolate city, my hut full of gear wheels

Golden gear wheels of fortune

Hundreds of miles of sea cling to my cheeks
thin seaweed sways restlessly
every day, my desire
thin seaweed, swaying restlessly by the stairs

You do not place coins on the round stones
frozen fish are swimming round
your raven eyebrows lean toward the dawn

3.

I desire the golden glint of your eyes
sun's goldmine
on a small island you herd your sheep

Your lips, the Red Sea

On a small tropical island you keep herding your sheep
among such lucid ferns, dragging an exhausted
whip, the sun cannot tighten its grip

Why don't I love the silver line of your nose?
centimeters of silver smile, with that beautiful
abyss beneath red azaleas
seashells and the everlasting night play a tribute to the morning

Do you hear that in the air?

That air praising me as I come from Rome
the ore beneath my feet, I am the god of bells

4.

The doors locked front and back
my hand reaches toward your breathing

Flies and old men on the street, scalding copper
in the noon heat, the dark night at noon unwilling to leave
his fingers, flames burning in the deep, lonely night
a night that belongs to the very end of dusk

My hands come together at your neck
growing in the cool wind of the mountain pass
without a sound on your gleaming precipice

So many books, season beyond stone

I turn lightly toward you

Wisps of my hair grow in the curling fragrance

Fall has arrived, bringing with it many leaves

25. Before Falling to Sleep

You cannot seize the leaves
cannot seize their sound

Things are changing rather quickly now
the sweet fruit bumps back and forth in the branches

26. Primary School

In the dark and dank afternoon

With all buttons buttoned

Silver flowers blossom on the blackboard

27. *Butterflies*

Field of pink
she's in the middle

Over there
facing here

Three designs of one springtime

28. *Burial Song*

Pounding small gongs, we greet the tombs
tooting little horns, we greet the tombs
the tombs have arrived
the little parade of tombs
carrying flowers
the little tomb parade

29. *Poster for the New Year*

Each peony blossom, so red it makes you feel strange
three blossoms all together

Plantain seeds washing the metal pan

Can you cover up the lizard in them
with your hands?

30. *Horned Toad*

I'll not tell anyone
not any sniper lying in wait
what happened out there on the dam

Women look at us
or don't
and they starch their clothes
swaying wolfberry trees

Red, white, and screaming prickly beards
fill the women nearby with unease

31. *Old Days*

Feeding every single face   shining   nightmares

32. *Adjusting the Frequency*

Throughout the country, craftsmen are repairing the dawn

Descending the mountain from the right   stars to the left
left of that, white-feathered merchants, and the large gear wheel of dawn

On one side, bean's purple blossoms, on the other, a purple metal
horizon

Hands pressed onto the narrow clock stand
those that we met have all disappeared

I recall some former lives
some copper coins of dreams

The bathroom light of dusk

Walking along the crumbling precipice, brush, and
crowds of people
with still miles of beach roads to go

And still some hope

33. *Blood Relatives*

She jumps up
and spits out a splinter
spits out the necklace of bones
above hangs a salad fork
and my wedding veil of days to come

Everyone sets their coffee on the floor
the nurse holds the boy

34. Book Cover

Everyone has their own tiny destiny
akin to the face of dusk
akin to the glow of chrysanthemums as they sway in the dark shadows

Theirs is such a gorgeous war

35. Wolf Pack

Light
inside the easy-to-open jar
traces of light along its inner wall

Someone covered with hair
in the flickering corridor

36. Creditor Rights

He retreats into the law

When he turns, the money
makes a noise

He retreats into paper
paper on the door

In the fragrant air, a face sways back and forth

37. Nature

I'm fond of that once-thrown spear
the ten thousand leaves in the tree
military troops crowding the earth

They show just their faces along the long, narrow road
ponderously waving their bird-nest banners
this is the subtle place where life fails

38. *In Respsonse to the Times*

That darkly colored lacquer tree
filled with green blossoms
I did not plant it
the small wooden building that stands nearby
I did not build it
smoke rising
where is my hatchet?
I'll write with silver
sitting at the writing desk
crunching numbers like fallen leaves
I have false teeth
the beef for lunch was delicious
outside the window the car blows its horn
I did not plant that lacquer tree
my whole life has been wasted

39. *Eulogy to the World*

She's always in the doorway looking into the gaping mouth of sunlight
a long and shining tongue
                    dragged across the floor

          The death of morning
                    a beetle falling suddenly from the bough

          A long and shining tongue

A car of splashy colors sweetens in the air, a gradual eulogy to the world

          A long and shining tongue
          morning's eulogy to the world

40. *Beginning of Troubled Times*

Cars drive hazily through the stand of trees
as if something were happening
a young child is led out from deep within the streets
where soldiers play a game of cards
when I fall scattered to the ground I see flowers
plumes of odd-looking smoke rising above the houses
twins they are
flowers sometimes lying for us in ambush
trampling us with their fragrance, this is a postcard of
time in, and not in, motion
spread with red, spread with green
        such a pretty child
        so pretty, looking this way
      the shutter takes a bite of someone
      shaking your head
      you forget how strange it is

41. *The Weekend*

Disaster like a box toppled to the ground
there are no longer horse carts in the town
there's not a bit of news, it grinds on by
turning us into fresh roses

There's nothing else left in the town

42. *Queen on the Coin*

Solemnly she sits in the middle of the sea
fingers tangled by the wind
she can't take her boat out for a sail

She is confined by the smallest of curses
a tongue like numerals curled

Alone she protects the delicate waves in the Gulf of Aden

She keeps thinking
that the person who loves her is chopping down a poplar tree
the tree carried into the boatyard, birds scream
the pistol cracks
the dream on the wet bar rattles on
and at that very place someone loses out to death

43. *The Soul Lives in Lonely Quarters*

The soul lives in lonely quarters
staring out at the warm wind below the hill
noting the lovely kisses
swaying like flowers
wanting to shake off the insect in its nectar
noting too the other kind of fallen leaves
scuttling here and there, blown by the wind
carelessly exposing their burned-out bodies

44. *Encounter*

Hair twisted in a bun, she pushes her bike

        The river's so very green
a rabbit hops about in the grass

Fire in the eyes of the dark gray rabbit

                You can ride a bike in the water
you can dry your ropes in the grass

45. *In the Afternoon*

If you go there
someone will be on the bus staring out
someone will be on the diving platform
looking down into the blue water
until the very end, body so red
and pockets so white

46. *In Conjunction*

When it rains
I coil wire at the window
the old man
sells fish in town
then I suddenly remember
the thing about the basket
a sieve that keeps the people out
so many times, thick and dense
squeezing, oozing
light red
rouge

47. *Afternoon's Silver Bracelet*

It won't be over even if this money is all spent
and we need not be worried and conceal our age
never understanding anything about this world
we treasure its fog and mists
our hats plucked off by gusts of wind

beasts stand elegantly by the wall
we cannot pick up our hats with our toes

48. *Tis*

Take hold of my hand
take hold of this jade
and put the comb away

The box will be smaller
come October

Over the Border

1984–1988

POETRY STOMPS OUT OF MY HEART

Poetry stomps out of my heart
off to accept its destiny
and alone, I moan on and on
the foot could have been kept there on the floor
but instead is in his face
and alone, he moans on and on
in the other half of the dream
we're busy again moving stones across the ceiling

Oil, from food left behind by demons
flows straight toward the open door
sunlight squeezes my arms together
the dream is a cave, don't go there alone
sunlight squirts through the fog
the old men and their streets
sit together in the sun, as flies crawl along
arms floating out of darkness, with their maroon and sovereign powder

WE LIVE ON ONE SIDE

We live on one side
of a gentle, sunlit valley
how can we observe
the sound of the snail's tongue
on skulls arrayed with thoughts
grass growing at the temples
little white fingers in a row
among them a sword, calling out
the sky falls before our eyes
teenagers out on the sand
in the rub, the sand finds its motion

the sky falls with a thud
on the sandstone, splattered juices

With my lover looking on, I close the window
and walk away from the light, toward the mountains
no flames in the sunlight
shadows falling on both sides

THE HOLY CHILD DESCENDS

I go out
in search of a bathroom
and see time there, unconscious time
serving well, with its clicking sounds
walking about dressed in white
a monster gnashing its teeth

Life is imprinted on the floor
and there are also stations and a driving staff
lawns in large swaths
maize, with the cool attitude of plants
imprinted on the floor
truth is a pretty little varnish

Sleep is a small jar
filled with warm liquid, daytime
is a snail climbing up the tall pillar of
history
stretched out
climbing straight toward the wall-light of winter

Behind me, a heavy layer
of golden velvet
what is termed flora of the feminine
not a bronze revolving door to be had
here, nothing can be seen
nothing imagined

Locked outside, my little brother
on a flight of concrete steps

a staircase under a clear blue sky
cries
without a sound he cries
he's knocked over his bottle of orange soda

MELTING POINT

Reaching a certain height the sun begins to warm us
but the rising and falling currency
will sink our dreams

Depressed, orange-colored bricks

There's no flower that can stand forever above the ground
There's no hand, no boat
no sound of spring water

There's no bird that can avoid the light of day

Just as none of us can avoid
ourselves
or the darkness

GEMS

The children scatter
                these precious gems
                soon to be covered with mud

The gems with their gray-blue lives
kissed on the forehead
                soon to be covered with mud

        Never to be found again

                The banners of the enemy appear
                the banners of the enemy wither

With the rising moon

A MISTAKE

I simply should've not been born into this world
the first time I opened that small box
a bird flew out, flew out into the shadowy flames

The first time I opened it

OUR DESCENDANTS

We can't help but sit here in the street
and welcome the ancestors of a murder
we can't help but array the pans, the bones, and the knives
shortening the hairs on the back of the neck
we can't help but sing military songs
wiping clean the ribs of sunlight
the table cuts through the water's surface

A stream of green blood flows
streaming green blood fresh in the cauldron

The left eye stares, nine o'clock, the sunlight brilliant

CROSSING THE BORDER

In the dust-covered street
it's God who lets you love
the bright and glistening sand
standing there, inspecting a handkerchief, it's
God who introduces you to the four of them
children, out of school, letting them
walk along beside you, giving you
clear directions, it's God
who lets you cherish the sand, pockets, and the children
holding tight to your hand to keep
the world from falling away

A wave, and another wave,
and the car
comes to a stop

THE GIRL AND THE RACCOON

Turning around, just once more
home is no longer to be found, home
is but a number, forgotten
it's lost, at home and a wall
and corn with its swishing sound
every home has this, open the door
every home has children, fresh
tops of their heads, every home has children
and me? In the construction site I catch
sight of a girl of cinders
with blue ashen hair
I climb the post to watch over her

DAYS GONE BY

These days are not crying days
you live in a house of rain
but when you come out, you are dressed all in red
or we could say, red is everywhere

The suitcase remains behind when you move away
it lies in the field
shadowy field of wheat, where green birds rise and fall

OVER THE BORDER

The flames in the many lamps flicker
                    Lei, my dear
I would go with you walking through snowy fields, silent in the storm

BRONZE STATUE

I stand at the lectern
lecturing to the distant islands
                no one round me

South Island, North Island

the white clouds linger there
the Maori use
knives of jade to shave

      No rain round me
for them I offer a blade to carve—glass, beards, and small letters
getting off one station ahead

Liquid Mercury

1985–1988

1. Names

Water poured from the stove
from the stove
        looking at her face   looking at the sky
      sawing the money in two   knocking twenty times
                      mist

Hauling West Gate with a cart, hauling it over to West Gate

               Ya
               Ya
               Ya

2. Eyes

More than twenty birds have disappeared
                              I suspect the cook
                              or the chair
• • Limping, limping
          the birds
            return   birds • encircle the pond
                          their beaks
                          trampled by ducks

Tie up the chair
        legs   sticking out   tie up the chair
                              •
                            Mountain
                            in extreme

3. Cottage

Just as it's getting light
I dream that I am standing naked, looking out

slowly sensing the east

On the other side of the glass, women there say goodbye
like waves disappearing into the sea

4. *Holding Still*

There's the ball
then the crowd
and then there are things in the past
the ship sails on
there is understanding   mending the night
a bed   alcohol   the swath of
gleaming business cards
holding in the wind
you come in with a candle
the one
student
who is late
shows you no respect

Scallions in hand
you watch how she picks up the ball so far away

5. *The Feel of the Wind*

The feel of the wind
reminds him of leaves
covering the lawns with biting lips
water-soaked lawns in
Shanghai
the hiss and slash of rain
covers the lawn
he keeps walking backward
listening to   the ringing, ringing
of little black beetles flipping over

        Morning   wedding
        biting each other's lips

Snow, snow white
blown backwards

Lifting oneself up
to see the new bride

6. *Writing Brush*

Days in the wind
       all grow their hair long
       let it rain
       and push the front door open
       arranging the wedding
       changing dogs   pigs   and chickens

       Changing here, changing there

       The eldest sister
       is a whip
       just now fallen in love
       fifteen   twelve   fourteen seventeen

7. *Red Wine*

Fooled like me

Always thinking that playing the flute
would bring you freedom
would let your stomach fly out from your loose and singing collar
silk so soft
on the small stage
arranging bottles in a row
with a stick, the lead singer must tap
                  the mouths
                  of the bottles
when evening comes, the lamp brightly shines
       bottles
       round
       walking
       toward   unable to speak with lamplight

8. Cord

Backing away   bitten by a
wolf

Sent to a field hospital
eyes   alert
seen by a nurse
threaded by a needle
watching the glass melt

Stitched up so carefully
you put on an act of having stitches
exhausted
sometimes, with all the coming and going, they catch a glimpse of you

9. Alert

Pink   guest

Two   blankets

Having said this
        lips full
            and moist
                leap into the back bedroom

10. Piled

Those stone-crushing politicians
can't get the fires in the stove to burn
into the stove they pile their stones
standing in the corner of the wall
listlessly   they smile
asking their old ladies to sing for them
their old ladies have won the support of many

Door to door they go
as they walk the streets crazed with excitement

11. Off to School

Off to school
eating grapes
and their seeds too
we spit them out
which is against the rules

And there is another student
book bag on her back
turning up stairs
into the classroom
she can't sit in front, like she should

Such is the afternoon
a dreadful teacher
painting hair
he paints from the middle
he likes to paint beginning with the brow

One twenty-year-old stands on the ground
the tree trunk's age
he likes to paint the shadows of
the afternoon
half done, he shows it to someone

12. Above is Only Sky

Above is only sky
a soft, soft, soft one

No need for you to make a turn
no need for headlights now
the mist floats back and forth across the road

No need for you
to bring a photo
nor words
or mist

A small patch of blue
sky
blue goes by

13. *Accident*

The roofs are buried in snow
and the snow covered with coals
seventeen hundred meters overhead
the sparkling begins

The lute says
the young are lutes
but do not pluck them
fondle them instead

Seventeen hundred meters overhead
suddenly it breaks away

14. *Devices*

This is the king you desired

Speaking to everyone
closing the window

This is the king you desired   a ladle lay in the snow

This is the former minister favored by the king you desired
          they say he   peeled   pushed along by water
          sparkled slightly crossing the street

These are your   troops
                    and small boxes
          that would sit, but cannot sit, on the concrete steps
     snap!

A thousand troops for light
                         snapping shut!

15. *Willow Jar*

With a small bumping sound
two people stand

> There is a city wall in the mountains
> there are trees near the wall
> there are women under those trees

Oh how their flowers   fade and fade some more
         eyebrows so delicate
         knives and clubs in hand

16. *Half a Peck*

Again we cannot find that broken
stove   or has the excavation already begun?
hearing its breath   below the ground
extinguished smoke   and rain
boots laid across its mouth

I must, as soon as possible, avoid thoughts of
grandmother   bound up by smoke
leaning to one side   looking   at the wall
with news pasted there   on the lower part
singing and spinning women at their wheels

Still when nightfall cometh I must
go down the river
to villages where the Great Yu excavated his fish

17. *The Great Clearing*

So many people watch you because
you will die soon, run over by a car right at
the next intersection, an intersection crowded
with people to whom you can say a word or two
in front of you there is still the accident turning your hair red
still you think about buying some books, you are a monster's child
dirtying your friend's clothes, you curse him

mom calls them down from the mountain
her hair is also uncombed, and black now too
you beg them to comb her
    hair
just to see the shining necks of others

18. *Help*

A frog spotted with old glands   a secret

    Really
           sometimes with such great care
adorned with the words "Longevity" and "Fortune" by her ears

19. *The Case*

We pluck the ripened fruit
we create things previously perfected

We pluck the already ripened fruit
       turning it lightly round
       shining with its curves
we create things already perfected
       rain
       and pillars in the hall

       Turning the handle back and forth
      drips and spatters   drips and spatters

       Swallows fly round and round you in the sky

20. *Hopes*

You see, no upper limit
you see, defeat by air

You see
       tons and tons   of standing
         little noggins

of air
seaweed
and salt water
the crops have all soaked through

Having seen this   move the former name around a bit

Five thousand mirrors reflecting the empty sea
when Anita relaxes her grip
she can feel death's apology

21. *On Occasion*

A sliver of landscape enters the yard
accompanied by
words
heads raised one by one
no one notices them crawling up the wires

Sitting there
reading
the wind-blown branches stroking everywhere
on faces   on shoes
in history books   everywhere

The daughter walks up from the first floor to the roof

22. *Manual of Sackcloth Prognostications*[1]

•

Who was that who came in with you
and who was that who went over there to talk
hanging on the stairs everywhere, hanging plates, fallen
in the snow a giggle
someone pulls tight   yelling plates

• •

Clothes washed now drying   slightly shining
a small mud brick
where did we see that little girl?

1   This refers to a twelfth-century Taoist divination text.

clothes with purple checks
clothes with checks seen before the thunder storm

    •

• •

Your letter is like a box to be opened
the wind polishes its four walls
four corners so silver
you sit sideways
sit sideways there a while   and then begin

• •

• •

Songs of mystery   songs of fishermen
                             for songs
     to live   live   live   and live
sackcloth prognostications make no sense
chasing billowing clouds into flight

23. There're Not Many Birds in the Village Now

    •

There're not many birds in the village now
not many at all
going outside to walk around

In the village there are some
and outside too

• •

Millet
falls to the ground
standing in the mud
cut down with a stroke
by the sickle in the wind

    •

• •

Pack full the rice basket for me

24. Writing

We write
like worms   finding their way through pinecones
chess pieces moved one by one
sometimes   for naught

Chewing on a word, contemplating its meaning
it tastes bad
threaded through with mildew
so we chew on another

We can't get there on time by driving
into the pines
seeds fallen to the ground
pinecones spread everywhere

25. Time

Round as a cup
mistaken
in our thoughts

With a light touch and light walk
placing things there
next door someone is talking

26. The One in the Sunlight

The one in the sunlight
has no tears
the one in the sunlight
cannot weep
the one in the sunlight
can only sit in silence
propped up by shadows
the one in the sunlight goes off to some place faraway
earth
rises high above

the one in the sunlight leaves with the tents
without moving
without speaking

27. *Men*

Shroud of apples
                            dining

28. *Whether*

> The second time they failed to calculate
> the correspondence of Christ's pain and sawn timber
> as explained

The narrator was my neighbor

29. *Liquid Mercury*

The mulberry tree wants to eat mulberries in the shade of the tree

he goes over there
nose lowered to the ground
the entire city watches the city

Don't try and trick him
smoke falling into the iron fence
the sobbing cockscomb blossom covers his face

Classmates are all in the mulberry bucket

Don't try and trick her
eating mulberries like this   fingers stained red
her skirt   spread out   fifty playing cards
here   there   everywhere
elder   elder   younger
brother   sister   brother

The mulberry tree wants to sew a skirt

When married they'll live in the mulberry tree

Fifty flags fluttering and fluttering some more

Rising earlier everyday   for
                                        a life of diligence

Steel bit drilling the mirror, drilling to the top of the trees

30. Ah Yes

Who can be truer than a bough

That red shroud hanging over the room

Leaving   leaving dishes

Hands
smile

Hands
dance

31. Borders

That's to say   those of tangled brush
                        are the other half
                        in the box I sleep
                        pressed to eat sweets
                        small lamps shine brightly
                        the wealthy are the other half

                        Today is the day he died
                        turning the white mountain over
                        I still have one more day
                        lamps light the runway
                        time   stretched on the line
                              sleep, oh, to sleep
                        half the day   is just enough

A half   slicing
                    a half
honeysuckle suddenly turns sweet   take a bite of paper

Plans approved but so difficult to put into practice

32. Homework

At noon   I am copying the staircase
one step
            and then another
written down
like this   whoever dies
is able to describe
how blood flows
how far from the trees
how much we are people in need of cars

Drawing
noon
heat
crossing the street

Gates opened wide

Yingying, our romantic heroine, trapped in language

33. I Hand You All a Knife

I hand you all a knife
you, my murderers
like flowers hiding their thorns
because   I have loved
fragrant times
midgets   and dwarfs   rank upon rank, troops turn the corner
with Pygmy hearts

Because I labored on the river bank
poplar trees sing to the very tops

Carve again those patterns　　Carve those patterns again
waiting until

The assassin's
love
brings its splashy death

34 A Warm Summer Day

I hold you tight　　crying
like holding a tree
never will I stop listening to
your pounding heart　　water-washed fruit
morning sunlight
washes through the corridors of the school

Arriving early
getting our grades　　choosing our seats
inside, the trees hide the light of the sky
the sun drops its red seeds
and deep in the bricks
draws out its flame

Inside, one by one the steles
have toppled over
their texts have toppled too
written in a clear hand
inside, the trees hide the light of the sky
inside, the steles have toppled over one by one

Still I'd like
to stand there　　counting
choosing seats
smoke　　spills, spills over
brew thee some tea
about face, mark time

35. *Benighted*

Entering
        the containers departed

Alone you watch the horse cart
alone you are two building blocks tormenting each other

Home
and
wok   father or son

36. *Home • Home*

No matter how far I go
I'll always return home
to touch the iron stove   the mirror
the tasseled blanket
and your hair

Always writing letters
of the distant blowing mists   how they blow

Curtains flapping in the windows of all the houses

In the streets always   such a large bird
wearing fronds of pine
melting me with its stare
melting   you
coming barefoot, singing barefoot

The painting
turning over and over becomes a sheet of white paper

Rocking back and forth it becomes a pond of blue water

Still I must write   how nice   holding you tight

        Smaller and smaller still
            drawing back

Smaller and smaller still
home   flees backward step by step

37. *Aluminum Oxide*

No one offered you a courtyard
where sometimes you'd see
pin-headed soldiers
standing beneath the trees

Apples fallen everywhere

A good many women
in seemingly good spirits
speak incomprehensibly
jabbering as they pass by
legs reflected in the water

Many flowers
two buds

38. *Smoking*

None of these flowers
should be of the mud
none should be of the dirt either
let the dirt miss her
let them leave the dirt behind
growing
feet as delicate as ginger shoots

No more dirt
no more thinking
let the women leave this all behind

The evening is filled with skirts blowing in the wind

39. Red Wheat

She sees her mouth hit the floor
she sees the bees rise and fall, up and down
there are many houses
hillside grasses from the hillside watch
she no longer has a mouth

She knows that smiles
are in the mind of the dead
sweet as examined throats
people who have died
seldom walk away alone

40. Dharma's Door

The lamps burn upstairs and down
all sick
with jaundiced light
inside someone says to you
yes,   Jessie   has left
                       little grain of rice
                       little country
                 go out and do something
                 do nothing
                       mincemeat

Powder on the walls and on the floor
powder hot
the flow of
hazy yellow light
Jessie   Josie
              the water is hot
                       go out

                 An hour
                 and a wok

41. Leroy

He stands there, face burned
feet hardened
he took Leroy on

Leroy died
so now he runs the court back and forth by himself
he was there
when Leroy died

On the court
sinking one of eight
people had him bet 50,000

He tore down the rim
running and swearing

Leroy scored one every minute

He took on everyone
they all died
but Leroy died too
that's how it came to an end

The papers reported

Boys who missed him wore his jersey
on which girls wrote   miss you, Leroy

42. Arrow

Just once she thought of this
cracks in the glaze like strands of hair
she washed the porcelain bowl
coming suddenly upon the blossom

She remembered the flower then
on the street
revealing just a little
of what was hidden inside the garden

Hidden sand   and dog
a large willow hung low
the noon breeze
blew through the wires

Each layer of the blossom
moved
with scents that
curled her toes

Fragrant flower   empty room
a person there
someone
that was the age of beauty

43. Telex

High into the sky
birds fly
my feet are tiny
pigs are pretty
wild boars hide away
spiked clubs
one mouthful
of oak leaves

                    red pig
                    green body
                    blue tail
oh yes
yes, that's it
the table should be small
so too the pile of dirt

44. Thoroughfare

The days pass by
small flags full of pins
there are a number of people pinned down
        it's over now   relatively happy
to take the opportunity to suggest

playing chess   people without legs
and people with legs all have beards
woven together
            one weave
can wrap up the room

Those in the room who can't get out
continue to play chess
grow beards
with ink brushes
draw on the wall   draw walls
draw rooms   people inside also draw
            a vista of a limitless space
            dots of white clouds   windows like rain
            the city has several places
            where girls from the city can go pick roses

45. Solar Flare

Wheat grows from the earth
and so do poets
you watch the whole body revolve
birds flying off ahead
the heart of the precious stone
vague teeth marks in the ground

46. Avant-garde

After an endless search
the jumping and leaping about
was his treasure

A pile of pale red and green cherry stones
was his treasure

Spitting a cherry out
he said, "Good"
was his treasure

Married, he ran away the very next morning

47. *Dee dee da dee da*

1.

Originally you could pass by
        clapping your hands
        walking across the lawn

Trees, bursting with leaves
you, bursting with words

Leaves

    Staying behind, you start the machine
bursts of bursts   bursting into smoke

2.

The overturned pail is seen from afar
        and dee da
      delicate fish
      dancing in the air

      Dee dee da dee da

Fish bring trees into the air
                    dee da

Fish bring trees into the
           air
        rust-colored legs sticking up in the
                    air

3.

Dee dee da dee da

      Trees pump out smoke   start the machine
                trees
                overturn
                setting fish free

Dee dee da
      rapping, rapping on the pail, looking for some money there

You   rip slip by slip   slip by slip
    until the crystal snout is exposed

4.

Dee dee da   dee dee da

      Turn the machine exposing the crystal snout
      a slip of a fish bursting into smoke

Five legs stuck out looking at me   at you
          we stare them down
          stare them down
          put them
                down

5.

Dee da   dee da
    the overturned pail is seen from afar
    machine starting fish
    a slip of white fish
    placed in the fish dish
    slowly slowly   dancing
                       into
                the evening waves

    Stare them down

6.

Rapping on the pail   looking for cash   and coins
                              like evening fish

Water flows down clear and fast

Down below   a bus stop   moving house
ripping
    snouts

Afterward, taking care of things   climb to the sentry post high in the tree
dee da

7.

Legs stuck out   inside
                watching
                fish
                in the wok
                rain

The whole afternoon is the windy season

        The dish speaks   dishes
                            dishes
                            dishes

You're the only drop to leap from the pool
            the only one
            dee da

        The door is open, always swinging back and forth

48. A Minor God

On the business of moving mica
you say four   then you say forty

Sea Basket Blues

1989–1991

PUPPET

Now   he has yet to begin
he's not drawn his gun
on you
you can speak
saying   how much you love the kid
big tummy, bumpity bump
holding tight to the small stool
    donkey cart
you and your sister, praises all around
his courage   like a corsage
grasping power
like a club
when you open the photo album
he walks across its pages

You never say you said nothing about yesterday
on the lawn
he came
giving his feet to you
       stretching his hand down
   saying
       my legs   my legs

You are an atrocity
electrified metallic orchids
force you to walk the road of purity
so poetry is what is pure

THE BOOK OF SONGS [1]

A small restaurant featuring chives
with seats all well arranged
has anybody come?
does everything look alright?
has anything been left behind?
go back and check

Everybody's gone
                all gone
            gone, all gone
still I want to take a look

VILLAGE AFFAIRS

Two Cart placed the residents in particular
Little Bubble placed Folksy in particular
and Folksy's brother placed the residents in particular again
then later someone with the last name of Feng
placed Old Ugly in particular
feeding them all radishes
and flowing tears

GOING TO WORSHIP

It is raining
fast-flowing blood

Next door they are building a house
built but then demolished

He watches birds walking along the road
watches birds greeting each other with a hello

Others watch him
with his black gunpowder holes

---

1 This is the name of one of the five Confucian classics.

YEAR'S END

He watches them toying with the door-gods

SEA BASKET BLUES

Just now, contemplating the price of silver jewelry
the beads above
ten for six ounces
                    or one for one ounce
the light came on

My former classmate is as tall as ever
when we happen to meet   clothes
                    are a little bit taller too

Plump and round like a little crow

You say she likes me
sitting in front of me
                    shorter than me   at the end of
class she gave me a handkerchief of glass

Look, along the edge   sixteen beads
                                    four forks
you really like those girls
who kiss with their eyes opened wide

SEEN

I see apples
when flowers are in blossom
seen from far far away
this single stretch of red

Fifteen birds are flying above the road
            flying by   but cannot fly away

WHEAT FIELDS

You look out at me from the crowd
having looked
you are very small
when you close your eyes   they are so blue

I know that you stand there inside some book
with boards up ahead

There is no way to know
spring   can't be seen   only once
all the flowers blooming
blooming everywhere

And later, so completely alone

THE BRIDGE

        Pulling layer upon and layer of branches back
you see the tree   standing there deep in sleep

FICTION

X.

The earth is a drop of blue water
within it breathes a faint flame

XX.

All you can do is to urge
the fish to sun themselves on the beach
and birds to sleep in the air

XL.

We were the ones to raise high the stars
and decided to gaze at them from below
though we wanted to live above them

L.

How could you have thought I was human?

LXX.

My dear
the earth has fallen again
at the time when life comes
you will keep her safe

THE GAZE

I.

They go upstairs
no one's there

When you open fire
don't forget the street of glittering flame

II.

Those on this side cannot go over to the other
and neither can those on the other side come here

None of the people crowded in the hallway can go to the other side

III.

This is true terror
burned-out houses
left standing like scraggly teeth

IV.

He stands up ahead
his collar red
you must salute
you must smile
you fret that you are too good-looking

V.

You are so frightening
smiling

Last time, it was not like this
LXXXIX
Year of the Snake

THE MARKET

Many people like to sing
some young   some old
some on a boat

When they begin to sing
the sea becomes woven with lines of foam

DUPLICATE NAMES

The tree is about to flower
but then, they look like leaves
and then again they're clearly flowers
leaves filling the mountains, filling the trees

        She's as elegant as fingers
        and a little shy

PIRATES AT SEA

If the big willow were to wreak some change
the children would be frightened indeed
counting buttons from one to nine   just like me
biking past the factory gate   I've not yet left
the sentry has lost his mind

THE SOUND OF A WINDOW OPENING

You hear
the sound of a window opening
in the distance is the sea

    The glistening boat
    lies in the dunes
    in the distance   is the deep blue sea

Listen
that whisper you hear   is the sound of the sea

    The boat lies in the dunes
in the distance stretches the deep blue sea

CHAIR

    The tiny sail   wrapping her tight
you do not let up

The rain washing over her   you spew your silk threads

      The flowers fall   she has a peach
      (I don't even know your name)

You'd like to be   taller than a flower   stem upon stem
      a little lower than a house

OMAN

    Under the wind blown sea
    there is a scuba-diving wife

    Inside the uncrackable nut
    there is the wind

    Under the undamageable roof
    there is a set of cards

Inside people who cannot love
there is the night

Under the staircase of soft fir that cannot be pushed
there are a foot   a clock   a stretch of waves
blown by the Second World War

SEPTEMBER

Repairing roads up into the mountains
I pick fruit for you
plucking that fruit   from dead trees
a hundred years ago   fresh fruit

I give you these   my child
                                        your hair
hangs straight to the ground   hanging straight down
raising your head
you slowly turn to me and smile

CALENDAR

One day   it blows hard
          and the roof rattles in the wind
one day   three evenings

One day we can see the church
               in the woods
               neat and tidy
     the sea reaching to the sky

One day   some fat guy
          is out there sunbathing for all he's worth

One day   we listen to the chicken's song
          while we tidy up the kitchen   it sings all day long

One day we think of nothing

One day we eat fish   nailing boards on the house
                         nailing all day long
        listen now
        this house is our sunshine

DUSKY RAINBOW

These are the wheat fields everybody knows
how well the wind blows
        like trees   toward the right
        like a horse
        seizing the girl who gallops by

Everyday there is one
every one alike

        Jia says nothing
        just like her father
        preparing the lantern for the coming night

WORDS

My dream won't last long
she has prepared fireflies

SEVEN DAYS

I hope there will be someone
to see me off
    holding my hand

The crowds of people on the mountain slope
block the sun from view

Two Sequences

1992

GHOSTS ENTER THE CITY—EIGHT POEMS

> The ghosts
> of midnight
> walk carefully along
> afraid to fall on their heads
> and change
> into men

Monday

Ghosts are fine folk
they sleep   then awake
they scan bulletins   go for a swim
standing high on the water
swimming out a stream of gold from the earth
flip fish   flip head over heels   blow on weeping bottles of wine
they like to watch things up above
and to catch, all at once, the golden
                              leaves

Ghosts too can sometimes read: "Indeed, they're well informed"
then place their hands underneath the document
"This old rose beside the river"
they say in unison   exhaling a cloud of smoky mist
at dusk people say
"It's time to go home"

Along the road the streetlights cast shadows
the ghosts don't speak   the wind blows through the streets
writing at the station   grazing   faces turning gray
a gust of wind rolls the mist away

Tuesday

Ghosts see people
with closed eyes   but not
with them open

A giggling kite
sometimes seen in a dream
now along the rail of the balcony
it falls   the ghost goes carefully down
and all through the hallway nothing but laughing
                                             kites

"Half for you   half for the others"
he unfolds clothes
looking inside   no one's there   he unfolds some more
a short blue skirt
"The   hospital   sala   slips into the water"
      fifth   room   mander
            he's surprised
      to see a large red fish staring back at him

The fish is now sick   written on a sign
the fish slowly opens his sweaty palm

Wednesday

Into the city on Wednesday
the ghost thought for a long while
                        with a
"crunch," he stepped on his own shadow
discovering he had punched a gaping hole
popcorn kept tumbling down
            adults five cents   children three
            just two for the little ones

Hastily the ghost squatted down mending his clothes
and mending the road
with a "crunch"   someone else punched a gaping hole
            the sound of singing surged upward

never to hear again the news of Jing Chunchun[1]
everywhere they erupted into parade
the prince began to bring in his winter garments
you stood on the bridge
                    beyond the moving cars, trains stop
"the metadefinition of affection is
in the very beginning I wanted to fight"
                    children
throw bottles here, there and everywhere

Thursday

The ghosts judge   the ballpoint pen
      twirling flowers
     three cents for a blossom

The ballpoint pen twirls around some adults
spinning them   into a round ball
then eating them
              she changed her name so there was no trace
the ballpoint pen ate one word   and wrote again

     Surname   Single
     first name   Full Lips
     the volcano is cold   it comes from the North
it won't do to just babble on, blah blah blah
one person spits out another   the tall get to talk

"Just three minutes left until the flowers blossom"
who asks   the air gradually becoming transparent
Someone   in the study is piling wash-
ing   off with the collar
the brush strokes are becoming ever fewer and the more
one paints   the fewer the hairs on the ghost's head

Friday

(He gets worse and worse)

---

1 A childhood friend who disappeared during the 1989 Tian'anmen incident.

pushing people   up the glass
    the ghost retreats
people, however, turn into pancakes
with mouths and faces   he dares not ask if he himself
has fallen   raised mouth, seeing the license plate on the side
the ghost reads
     one horse
     five clouds   five soldiers

Sandwiched in a book a horse yelps   at the same time he noticed
the square-jawed writer and the fluffy brain above

     Five horses   five soldiers
          walking back   making
   the balance   balanced   **to balance**   five armies
     (so hopeless, wherever he goes)

That's a chess set from the north
grapes wither   soldiers are heroic   flowers flourish
the first time he broadcast the news program was in the movies

Saturday

The ghost
is in the movies again
           Popcorn Revolution   that's the title
people beat up on him
he says   be brigade leader, be division commander, that's fine
     but not commandant of the army   that's for me to be
     don't try and deceive me
     a troop of soldiers is passing out gifts on the ground
     everybody knows   when the red plum blossoms
     changing from green to red, she is on the other side
     needing someone   needing to need negotiation
     why is the flower so   red?

First: register for marriage
     if you change your name, change your nickname   with a pen
second: students lift their benches   into the sky
     thrown   but not thrown like this

we need three to stand on benches and throw ropes into the   sky
thrown well   they can be kites

Third: giggling
with a laugh   the director fills the air with enfolding mists

Sunday

"The dead are the beautiful people"   after saying so, the ghost
looked into the mirror   and he was actually only seven inches tall
     he was pressed down by a pile of glass   the glass
          brushed clean
"The dead are all pretty"   like
     glass without shadows
     white projection screen   lit by lights
     passing through the slides   layer upon layer
the dead are at the emergency door
a huge pile of glass cards

He stuck his finger in one nostril
the light shone   he stuck it in the other
shadows cast by the light, the city disappears from sight
 —she still cannot see—
you can hear the sound of bricks falling to the ground
the ghost is very clear
the dead make the air tremble

there are stars far away   and farther still
there are stars still   only after a long while
did he know there was a transparent poplar above the chimney?

Spring Festival Day

The ghost doesn't want to do the backstroke
     bulletin!
the ghost doesn't want to fall on his head
     bulletin!
ghosts won't become men   bulletin number seven   ghosts

     playing a lute   relaxing

ghost   **ghost**
            no faith   no trust   writes letters   turns on the lights
            no love no hatred   **eyes**
ghost   **all at once**
            no dad   no mom   **open**
            no son   no grandson
ghost
         not dead   not alive   not crazy
                   not stupid   just now the falling rain
                      put in a bowl, one look
                      and he knows those blinking eyes
            ghosts swim under water
                                        seeping through the deep
         the conclusion is
only on the diving board does the ghost fall from grace

CLASSICAL TALES FROM WAIHEKE ISLAND—
EIGHTEEN POEMS WITH ILLUSTRATIONS[1]

1. Lord of the Island

The lord of the island dwells on his isle, scanning the skies. In days past he bid his time in the mountains, yearning for the sea. Then, quite unexpectedly, above the South Pole the ozone layer was breached, and, with the melting of glacial peaks, the ocean waters rose. Thus came baleful bother to the one of his desires.

With a sigh he says: clouds in the sky, people on earth: people who are penniless, working without stop.

2. Switching Husbands

Husband-switching sisters are transformed into a painting, with winds and percussions; feet swimming, heads blossoming; a small palanquin comes to pack the girl away. The girl speaks: A girl is, at heart, a flower. What kind of flower? A penniless flower.

---

1 Gu Cheng drew eighteen illustrations to accompany each of the prose poems. However, a selection has been made for this edition.

3. Fishing with Torches—A Painting

The painting "Fishing with Torches" was done with the approaching night; as she of beauty was falling into sleep, there was the shimmering of a glimmer of light. Suddenly the candle burst, wax flowed forth, and the flame leaped a full foot, forming a huge wick. So I trimmed it, and did this painting.

Thereupon I penned: Fish bear the water, water bears flowers, and flowers bear a fine family.

4. Good Works, Good Discussion

Good works are good for discussion, preferable to not discussing; in fact there's nothing to talk about.

The song goes: Only moms are precious in this world; kids with moms are like pearls.

5. This Idiot Proposes

This idiot proposes, wrapped in a wrap, lifting a small bell, looking into the dusk, ringing, ringing . . .

The bell rings: That vamp, that little vamp, that . . .

6. This Idiot Gets Engaged

This idiot gets engaged; cheers resounding like thunder claps, knocking over the belle in a fright, and banishing the neighbors. There is only one couplet that captures this mood—
  The first line: No dad, no mom, no education
  The second line: But food, drink, and your old lady

7. Fishnets Flying through the Sky—A Painting

Fishnets fly through the sky snaring the beauty. She is transformed into a small bug flying, the fishnet into a huge eagle, its call sobbing.
  Earth like a pot, heaven like a lid, heaven and earth together are a dish to be ordered. Why must one distinguish between main dish or side, salad or stir fried, julienned or diced.

8. Discourse on Fish in the Old Temple of Shrine Mountain—A Painting

Ancient disputations refined, contemporary bull; we stray into the dense mountains, dreading naught on any side. Sometimes we discuss people, or things, or news, or scandals, or beautiful women, or cannons, or novels, or egg rolls; gods on high, cash down below, there is nothing on which our words do not touch. Moreover, beyond the window, ancient trees luxuriant and a sea without limit, thus we do not make days and nights our care; clear-eyed when awake, sleeping when fatigued, passing the years as if they were days.
  One evening, getting fish from the sea, we salted them. The chef stated his plight: The salt I have eaten is greater than the rice you have partaken. The listener was stunned and said: How can it be that you have eaten salt of such proportions?

9. The Bird of Paradise Gets Its Way—A Painting

I reside on my island, scanning the skies; near the southern horizon, it is everywhere empty and vast; occasionally birds in flight take their rest under the corridor eaves, perfectly contented couples. Eating a seed, unaware of the schemer, mouth red and body green, cheek feathers as pristine as snow, it flies off, mile after mile, the sound of whistling wings.

The song says: In mountains and in seas, in rivers and in lakes, two trees do not a woods make, and I lose myself in fields; rain water for drinking, brushwood for fuel, there is a daughter at home, but no neighbor on his high horse.

10. Heaven's Will—A Painting

Friends came from afar and returned to somewhere far away. The letters come and the letters go. The poems come and the poems go.

The poem, a gift; the Gatha says: A whisp of cloud in blue skies, travels a myriad miles without design; thus one whispers, traveling a myriad miles, there is no whisp in those miles of sky.

11. Double Bottle Rocket into the Sky

Double bottle rocket into the sky, reduced by a half; one half exploded, the other only smoke, one half a flower, bird, bug, fish, a lucky marriage.

With a sigh, I say: But nobody saw it.

12. Hair White as Snowy Skies

Living long in the mountains, no snow but blossoms: such homesick longing.

Again reciting: Hair white as snowy skies, whiteness by the handful;

others say snow is snow, but I say no, snow is blossoms. Fine flowers fine for the guests, good snow good for going home.

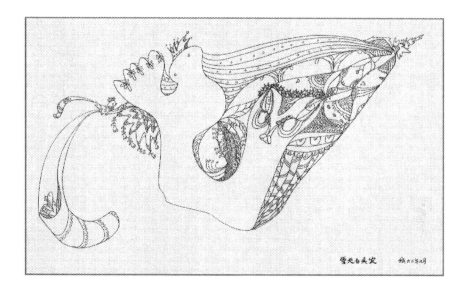

13. Baldy Stirs Up Trouble

Baldy is not that bald at all, hair hanging off one side. Feeling chilled, he tossed the flower and cleared the grass, severed the water and uprooted the wave, taking this as heaven's will. Those who met him, all hated, detested, blamed, and ridiculed him, hating his vulgarity, detesting his abandon. One night he entered the mountains; with the cluck of the chicken, he was enlightened, transformed and gone.

A Gatha inscribed in a hat, half riddle round:

The Gatha read: The chicken embraces its coop, the monk in meditation, spirit moon shining, chicken egg of the heart.

Another reading: Chicken and egg, monk embracing his coop, meditating spirit, shining moon heart.

14. Sun's Self-Immolation—A Painting

A myriad miles from home, with nothing for my livelihood, I began to throw pots made from clay unearthed at South Mountain, and had black vessels, a full load. On to the market with them I went, and sold none at all. So I went to sojourn at South Mountain, at the Temple of the Fire

God. The monk said the god is magnanimous but meticulous; if thou stay, then stay, but no ranting away. This I took to heart. Off I went to bed without a sip, but in my sleep I chattered carelessly, offending his spirit. The god brought down flames from heaven, brightening the night like day, and destroying my pots in his fury. The mountain wilds illuminated in an instant, magpies flying up time and again, only I slept without fear.

With dawn's first light, the monk knocked on my window, and then I knew that my load of wares had become piles of goblets, glazed with golden stars. How weird!

The gazetteer records: And after three hundred years, the immortal temple was seen no more, the sand jar installed on the upper dais, the earthen cauldron through corridored mountains; during the day, a screaming madman; at night, a wife and child providing sustenance; in the morn it is said they still are not fired; at dusk it is forbidden to return the money.

15. What There Is to Regret

My friend, Yaping, likes cigarettes and booze, and likes books of Lao and Zhuang, and the military tomes of Master Sun too. He listens but says nothing, drinks but is silent, only a smile. One night he foreswore drinking, then up and threw a book across the hall, saying: Laozi and Zhuang-zi are both sons, Sun is a son too. But what of the sons of these sons?

Startled I replied: Always try to adopt a faux posit-son.

The Oracle reads: If, with a petty heart, we calculate a petty belly, each calculation will be exact.

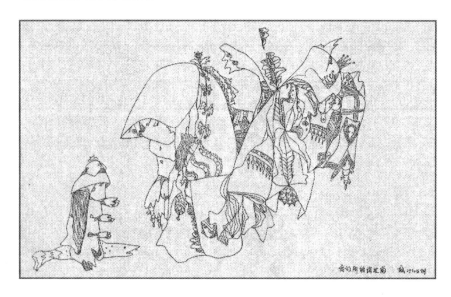

16. Homesick—A Tune

The garlic of old is fully cloved, and for breakfast a wide bowl, sweet sauce for the noodles, scallions for dipping, sliced cucumber, and a fried egg too; no matter that they are spicy or plain; but nice and slippery, crisp and crunchy, slurpity slurp, pulling without stop, ladling without end, twirling round and round, and sucking on and on, rolling into balls, one bunch after another; good for the heart, good to taste, good for thought, good for life; nine meals in three days, for holidays, for the New Year, for birthdays, or for just growing up; ground pork, sesame oil, chili peppers, black pepper, dried shrimp, wine vinegar, hotbed chives, all fried with some sort of dried clams; crisp and tasty, all in a delicious muddle, Saucy Noodles with blended flavors.

The customer calls: Check, please.

17. The Stone that Did Not Fall to Earth

Duke Ford, thinning hair and missing teeth, each time he peered into the mirror, smacked his forehead and informed the glass, if my hair continues to fall out, I will turn thee on end.

The Coda reads: The mirror can be turned on end, but one's head cannot be turned on end, if one's head is turned on end, then so is the mirror turned on end; if both mirror and head are turned on end, then it is as if they were not turned on end; it is but the world that is turned on end, and in the end, what is one to do about that?

The strategy: Perhaps the head of the mirror can be turned on end

The challenge: That would be only an upended mirror/how could that reveal an upended man/unsure whether a man is mirror/yet claiming the mirror resembles a man/a man into a mirror can peer/but a mirror only peers at the man/they say the mirror is a void, in the void only the man is revealed

Singing: How wonderfully wonderful/rising up to Western Paradise and not coming down.

18. Heaven's Pure Soil

Suhua, surnamed Li, lived in Vietnam for years. While young she was caught in the fires of war, and cast upon the sea; she drew near death several times. In the end she came to study in Germany. Her kindness to all she met, a scholarship happened upon, spread among her classmates; without a trace, they received from her but never knew. A long time hence, lodged at South Seas Mansion, just as I was discovering that a woman's nature is like heaven's pure soil; something to know, see, understand, and judge. I sought her anew, but, as it turned out, no one knew her whereabouts.

Longingly they say: The wind is without shadow, and water without shape, but when the swan lands in the snow, the true traces stay.

This spring, I write in honor of her.

The City: A Dream Sequence

1991–1993

When I arrived in Germany, it reminded me of the Beijing of my youth. There was the snow and there were the bare branches shaking in the wind. I sensed that if I were to go for a walk along the streets that lay beneath my window I would return home, where I could once again see West Gate. The dusk's desolate light cast the crenelations and surrounding wall in looming silhouette, as the sunset bled across the sky.

In my dreams I often go back to Beijing, but it has nothing to do with Beijing of today. It is a place that is heaven-sent just for me. Peace Lake and China Gate are now gone; also gone are the bricks in the bright sunlight, the cinder road along the hillside, and the wild jujube trees. And yet, I still move above them, looking down on all below and on days to come.

There is one thing that I know and although people do not talk much about it, they occasionally let something slip. This thing that I know is about me. I know that this is what makes me, no matter where I am in the city, unable to find an escape. Standing somewhere, gazing out, all of a sudden I can recall nothing. Yet there remains this vague feeling that somehow stays with me. A thing that continues, like when I was a child and would reach out with my hand searching for chalk in a very long corridor—this corridor might turn into the Long Corridor of the Summer Palace—my hands are always reaching out, whether in protest or surrender I do not know. This is a thing I bear alone.

My poem says: "Following the river, you want to go back/tickets, each one a dime." I had difficulty rowing on the river . . .

I have written only half of the poems in this sequence "The City." Many gates have yet to be covered. But I want to send you these to look over; maybe they are a new version of the Ming novel *Dream Visits to West Lake*. I do not know. Often I find myself just singing a line from a Vietnamese folk song: "Oh, sad town of mine . . . "[1]

—April 10, 1992

---

1 This preface was a letter Gu Cheng wrote to his sister Gu Xiang.

1. China Gate

Every morning, ice and snow
four of them all together
she always rides her bike on the side of the road
the children tag along, messing with clods of dirt
thus the road is finished

Someone who knew her said
come to my house
does she still paint?
so well-behaved   no matter who it is
when she's tired

No, it's not like that
you need to grind your ink   a little bit slower
eat   slowly grinding
she said
waiting for her own seat

She's just fine

2. The Temple of Heaven

From the busy intersection she looks in my direction

                                        extremely well-built

She's far away from me   as if leaving a morning tree

3. East China Gate

There were so many cheap things in the yard
and you were cheapest of all
running here and there   making the queen get dressed
she said   you shouldn't be like this
in a while we'll go for an operation

There were so many maids in the yard
wanting to go back   they crowded the railing
the unlucky one was the glass

she leaned over to look in the mirror   the queen said that
her schoolgirl looks were disgusting

Someone drove a water truck into the yard to fix the glass
he   was of two brothers
so young
under the steps   even younger   she
just back from the States   do you want to see the paintings?

In the yard   most important is the furniture
he didn't understand   why so many chewed holes
were still being mended
the building was built up like this
sixty dragon chairs   selling for   two hundred pennies

In the yard within the yard   you were in no hurry at all
you can't count clearly even a little change   count you
the money was built up like this   once worried
then you move the table
saying   just let me do this for you

4. *Meridian Gate*

I have been looking, all along, for that stone
to sharpen my knife
                    she is too soft
                    to be broken apart

Sharpening knives   three people sharpen   the square

                I watch the butcher
                    hold the knife
            he has me make a folded swallow
I show her the glass chess set   saying
off with his ears   she is upset
pushing a goblet over to me

                        At the next table

            The knife holds a hand
        too soft   without a sheath

two knives   cut down to fifteen dollars
fifty-five to fifteen   sand
stone   fifteen men run   too fast
        they have to return

All the stones are of your choosing
give them each a suitcase
in   a golden horse, silver colt blue suitcase

               Moon light   so bright
                 fifteen   of them
have all been tried on the green tablecloth

5. *Victory Gate*

Too much earth   is never good   dirt on all four sides
sunk in the middle   the only way to build a house is to dig

The dragon was originally a beautiful woman

Actually, one hundred and ten beds   everyone there chose one
when they came back   the lights were on

But God commanded to have the dragon

They say all this so that you could finish getting dressed
    look carefully there's still someone else up there

Made into a beautiful woman—for

She showed you around the back alleys   saying there was
someone who died here   they grew even older

Ever and ever

Still at work you must have not seen this place
               circling   a grave
    Feng   how did you know her name?

6. Kiddo

Going into the sunshine
the ocean has a tail

we still have much to learn

7. South Pond

There seem to be some faint sounds
        placed all around   by birds

There seem to be some marbles in the drawer
the flower pointed   and much enlarged

It seems that when we came   they said
        the flower is a dog
                        the flower wants something to eat
                                        (going out the back way to
the grocery store   just to look around)

Flower   flower • dog
a large mouth   opening hungrily on a leg

8. Back Bay

They watched you
they were not wearing clothes
you did not feel it lasted long
you were not wearing anything either
I said there would be other programs that night

I put my hand under my shirt
one of my knives was gone
I didn't believe leaving would be like this
the knife was too short
I let you walk on ahead as swiftly as the wind

The most annoying thing about committing murder is finding the
    opportunity

she caught up with us
                                  what the hell was she doing
I stared at her in the hallway
girls cannot be killed

But yesterday they killed four
two in the bedroom   two at her door
you showed her the knife
saying   you were going to die
she smiled   asking you how many kids you had

      Following the river, you want to go back
      tickets, each one a dime
      standing up   you
      they are going to take their seats
      you alone are thinking about the scenery at the station

9. The Emporium

Look waters in the suburbs are rising   stores of bronzes
mountains in clouds four Tang horses   round the mountain, past the shoes

At the counter   you help me suggesting
that I go   look at a vendor's stand
later you did not speak again   but in the morning you did
you know them   looking over two stands   in the evening
you did not speak again   the morning was cold

You went   you knew what to guard against
she asked you to sit down   but you didn't
you needed to return   up ahead was a crowd
together we came here   and together we go
there is no price for which you would sell   me

Two places to go   a school   on the road
put down the bike   trees are sprouting   he bends easily
in the past   people combed their hair the other way
on the bus you keep talking
      to me
I gave you so much   but none was green

Together mouths turning green   you did not know
to ask for less   the bear pushed on the door   so warm
people in the distant past

Laughed at undying fire   what's with all the noise

        Big mouth, big mouth goldfinch
        altogether   more than seventy yuan

10. The Capital Theater

On Saturday   she says   kitty kitty
somewhat after three   she says   kitty kitty
                             kitty kitty   kitty kitty

        Tiger does not budge

(3)

            12 people at the table
with strawberry candy and apple tigers   the call-to-arms just right

            Let's run away together
(7)

These days you pay too much attention to that flat face
                        keys
actually   as soon as the water's hot   the horse drops
the thinner the legs, the longer the legs, and the easier they drop   how
    can they not?

(11)

At the meeting on Saturday   look
                        gold and silver   the stripes of tiger and fox
the crew of 12 look   where it's at
            if you want to take pictures you'll have to bring a little water

(5)

This is a small cat
rummaging the tiger cloak   you look at yourself laugh   he looks at
himself laugh
                    everybody is laughing
              the girls all laugh they're not tired

(13)

Gingko buds   in the middle of the day
                        she follows her   she follows him
              up the gingko tree
        somewhat after three   she said   they all are

(1)

Somewhat after three   the lamp was not lit
      they only ate a bit
                              the lamp couldn't be lit   how could it not light?
she sits on the bed   thinking about the way you live

(9)

        tell   the monkey   to go pass the flower halls
                        no, that's not right
the cat passes by the flower halls   in the coal fields passing by the flower
      halls   beating   wasps on the bodies of tigers
        monkey, oh monkey, passing by the flower halls   in the coal fields
              passing by the flower halls

(15)

      Why do you now stop
                        drilling through
        the room is near

(17)

Passing by flower halls on the bodies of tigers   in the coal fields beating
      wasps

monkey, oh monkey, beating wasps
in the coal fields passing by flower halls
beating wasps on the bodies of tigers

11. The Palace Museum

How nicely they have repaired the windows
   it was his relatives who repaired them
altogether two doors   that the bird called four
            with eaves
originally nice looking

   The relatives all knew   • first to pick up the bench
I knew too • why it had failed

12. Xidan Shopping District

Let me look   two times it will be the street
once for resisting the Japanese
once for promoting hygiene

They hold lamps
the night is dark and misty   you may come out

Go read *Week in Review*   the clock tolls the hour at Liubukou
looking in the shops   familiar
staircase   several pages of critique
critique of the army   prose of praise

They all hold lamps
between the buildings

It seems that it's all in order to make you happy
standing still   throwing bottles   let her run away

People seldom throw bottles at the gate of their own factories
                     waiting for a proper time

Three elder brothers, sixteen younger   everyone knows them
most people know them some   juicy oranges

13. *Shops at Xinjiekou*

Dummy is a lotus flower
dumb now   and held in one's hands
hands that cannot be exchanged

14. *Black Bamboo Park*

In the water, going back to the city
        the television is blue, so blue
(why in hell didn't they take care of this as they
should?)

Today is your day
working in the hallway
        your brother's job
        tooting his flute in the dark
        his thing
you'll leave soon

You'll leave soon   there's no water

    (You said water cannot be held in one's hands)
there's no water
        about to leave

The shadow bumps me
the shadow says you play a flute in the dark with someone else

15. *The Oil Painting*

The withered tree can also cleave
the mud speaks
saying that you have caught up to the shadow in the wind
coming down with the wind
her tree   gave her flowers
her tree stands only in the sky
her baby can only stand

There are also branches here like these

16. Six Mile Bridge

A tree of long standing   the bay bends
     now toward the policeman
throwing sand
thrown layer upon layer   on the police box of Xidan

     Arriving at Xidan in the morning   forty
programs jumping back and forth   chairs   red
     reporting to Secretary Zhou   the lieutenant sergeant
     goes back home in the snow
     snow covering the glass

     Like paintings
snow   snowing heavily   needing a thousand sheets
white paper fleas   cannot live
     look
     chicken pecking chickens
     beaks gobbling beaks
     temple returns to temple
thirty-five military rules   pulling out nail
     s

     Good morning   from Factory Eighty-one to the bay by bus
     east of West Gate   seal the gate   can live no longer

     Friday having oatmeal and tea
     Xiao Mountain athletes   white paper fleas
holy ghost

So exciting, the jumping back and forth, the horn grows smaller

     She's on the mountain
     very tall   very small   like a nail
     taking aim
the mountain is very small   very tall   very dark   trees

White paper fleas
     it snows the whole day
the bus stops at the bay
     sawing the tree
     into pieces round and round

(Let's clean up the remaining branches)

17. *Zhongguan Neighborhood*

When I find the key   I write

Going to the 5th floor of page 52   to read
                                                                        Science Illustrated
dig a spoon into fruit
                                looking at the surging sea
        ice on the cabinet
        (I can only believe you stole it)
open
the door   over   over and over   over
                                                and over
the bicycle goes on up   go take care of the papers

            The   fixed
            bicycle   the bent   the size was wrong
            repair   aluminum
            shop   key
                                                you're the smallest one

18. *Cut and Paste*

So much of a good time
        flowers
        your people are in the trees

        So many small factories
flowers
your people are in the trees

        Copper-clad nails
        nail heads
        green goats

    Flowers
your people are in the trees

Fifteen feet above the ground
jumping from the northern room

old men of distinction
one bullet each

Flowers   heads bent down   feet pointing up

19. *Colored Ink*

I'm picking apples from the smallest tree
    will you come down
    and show me
                the purple edge or the yellow edge
                the purple edge and the blue edge
                the purple edge and the blue edge

The painting worth being painted is composed of water

20. *Changping County*

Done with painting   smear the green grass
he's embarrassed
not to die   the bouncing ball

There's something good about a bouncing ball

Don't turn the table over
whatever you say, it won't be
grab him from above by the collar

Salad fork   butter-knife

He's embarrassed
at this point in time
needing to teach the children to paint the glass

Things of the past have gone ahead

Never to die
he needs to paint the glass
            meow
neat and tidy   grass of glass

21. *The Peking Public Library*

Climbing is not a thing in the past
at this time   the station is turning from China toward the scenery

22. *North Street, Altar of the Moon*

A moment ago this crew   still had people
                    then there was not a sound

      The flower opens like a large net
                    shaking the departing shoes

23. *The Mail*

Okay   it's late now   Chrysanthemum will come tomorrow
writing you letters   people from every unit will come
every square will present fresh flowers
                                        sinking
      the sound of the sea behind the main mast
I wonder it is alright   please offer him our gratitude

24. *The Princess's Tomb*

      They said   it's cold
      but what is the form of this coldness
I do not know

They have presented flowers
            out in front of mother's place
            on the small path toward home
                        presenting flowers
            for fifteen years
the trees look tall and strong

25. *Spring Pavilion*

A corridor so very long   and chalk there

      Reaching with my hand so high

26. White Stone Bridge

I thank the courtyard   for birds in flight

When I arrive   they sleep all night in their clothes

27. The Polishing Factory

Cold and dead   no firing of what should be fired
she's outside the house laughing

28. Feng Terrace

Fire burns in   it's true silver
is there really a Marco Polo Bridge?

Now you have both light   and people   wading through mosquitoes
        on the road ahead   together they sing

29. Peace Lake

When fishing you should be careful of the rising river
        water with no one in it
your bag is in the boat

    When fishing you should be careful of the rising river
    (go to where the money is)
                    water water everywhere
your bag is floating in the boat

When fishing you should be careful of the rising river
    the water gone
            your bag is floating in the boat

You're still young   you don't believe you'll ever be old or alone

30. *Fated to be Together*

On the plane she said
    she was going to die   **King of Heaven, red freckles of jade**
no more meal tickets   but he can still cop a meal
fish   of the sorts that dangle from key chains
the newspaper sprawled open   **in front of the eight-horse door**
at the railing   are people wanting there to be people to say there
    are people
        and there's me wanting there to be   **more people at the door**

        In Ying's hand
        an apple has   **been**
        chewed while being
        waved
            united
after this
she moved dishes about **in a** restaurant   reading the weekly prices
    so very high   **good** that everyone's weekly concern is **marriage**

Exchanging them all for young girls we know

31. *The Eastern Mausoleum*

Dusky dusky wheat   the weather this year
    is shrouded in newspapers   just as you said
    but, ha   the biscuits are so hard
        what are things of cotton and silk   they will do
        she eats only the freshest food   thirty-five stations give on to the idea

        Thinking how laid back   mind elsewhere
            sometimes a goat lifts a bottle
        to discover "Qi" on the neck of the knife rack swallowed up

        What is said just now does not matter   what is said just now
                        to fish with pure iron
            caught
            the screwdriver raised
                then
                hanging

hapax
lego   menon

Drill the hole a little smaller

32. Ping'an Neighborhood

I always hear the nicest sounds

You can turn off   the light in the hallway

33. Bridge at Tiger Workshop

Tiger walks back and forth along the road
see   things aren't that great
a cat under the window   face raised
looking at sunflowers
suddenly you take out that cats-paw
and the trays of the scale fall upon the ears of wheat
the ears of wheat are falling   but the stalks stand
and Elana, a painter from Sweden

Suddenly they chop off its head
that's one-third   what can one say to a rat?
they dragged it over there
and brought back a hairy coconut
one cut under the street lamp
you advised him   told him   this time
they'd snap off his legs
hair also grows inside the little coconut

<There are so many golden days here on the earth>

They are out back walking out back
<golden flowers wave in the breeze>
you leaned forward with a sudden smile

34. White Pagoda Temple

The Three Mile River of the Yuan
was within my domain
Beany said it wouldn't do to repair the narrows
but rather the ballad of the Red Flag
the facing bathroom to be whitewashed
several people stand on the pagoda
of Red Flag's north station
laughing loudly
the sound of smoke   several people
standing atop the pagoda

In a room of Red Flag's northern station
painting the Red Flag Ballad
several people hold up the flag
so the rest can rasp it away
she keeps on laughing   keeps on
laughing that no one else can hold onto water bent
and measured with a ruler from the drawer
with the sound of smoke   she said
don't get burned

He is of the Yuan Dynasty
we belong to the Jin
still using a brick as a stamp
the ashes from the stove spill out
let the one living upstairs come down   laughing
why are you laughing?
the one living upstairs isn't your dad
        still she laughs
all the flowers of her home have turned white

35. Temple of Earth

The opportunity to emerge   is of the purple stones
        and also to enter
                                        she is startled
open door   in the shade of the trees

36. *Hall of Cherishing Benevolence*

The Chinese Revolution   is pasted on the wall
in an office across the way
    one person, one group

It seems fine to me

                (it's fine   but not too much)
In fact
I would have you
stand there in the train
                clacking
                and clanging
    the train is leaving   he is leaving too   down the next set of stairs

37. *The Marble Boat*

Turn around   look into that mirror of yours

Its canopy so decidedly dark

38. *The Bell Tower*

        It's raining   tie those laces

            Watery green glass

        What's with you and the fish bowl

The little old man is running round and round the bend
a northerner

39. *Winged Red Banner*

I would nail down the roof with roofing nails
surrounded all around by velveteen trees

40. Willow Street

At midnight, across the bridge, in the rain
emerge the Army engineers

41. Flowers for a Present

You said how white they were
and also a little pink
but this time they are yellow   the color of unbleached cloth
like the lamp beside your bed

42. National Gate

You can't relight the sun
smothered in ashes from the stove
people to come   holding to a string of railroad ties

The first time, a layer burns
the second time, it explodes
                    as soon as you slip in you feel
                              something's wrong
dust turning white even without fireplace tongs

(Bandits wounded) (grief unfathomable)

43. Ganjiakou Neighborhood

Winter, you see
                    is so long
without a haircut
      one person
            open fired
      along the mirror into the inner room

Last time each and everyone
                              exuding sweetness
dyed a swath of the
red satin comforter

asking if there had been buses by
    the   335   or   336

The 336 is loaded with people
at the last stop
              changing lines
    not moving
        buses
are all digging ditches in the yard
    from twelve o'clock till
        lined up in a line

Each and everyone gulped wine
    and returned home
the cotton flannel wrapped around the fluorescent light
    at twelve thirty
they say   to burn down the street
fluorescent light and corduroy
          riding pants

From twelve o'clock to twelve o'clock
    no one is allowed
      to light a cigarette
        by the courtyard gate

    Such is the fate of each and everyone

Faces, each and every one, covered with a white cloth

      The road is reflected in the mirror
      the road turns
      flowing cows, horses, and carts reflecting flat faces
they have beaten what ought to be beaten
and soldiers   are still here watching
      each and everyone working

44. Huicheng Gate

Going south
more dazzling than poplar leaves
you would go north

Women along Longevity Road
stare at your long wiry beard

45. *Elephant Street*

According to future orders
Dusty is to be exhausted
he will burn down the kitchen
    cut open the window
while wearing army fatigues

    Gorgeous said
the third hall   and second factory
are exhausting
one half of them incinerated
and of you there, who's going?

In July the guns were loaded
none can be trampled
the skin of the cat rolled
    several times
taken down laughing   hung up coughing

    A soldier of the highest caliber
    captures dragonflies
    he can greenly afford
    white lightness
he twists the little centipede rope

What is this?
Master Guan of fine moral fiber
    would not kill someone
but he still isn't very clear
how the flowers on the grave became towering trees

46. *Temple of Myriad Springs*

Go ahead, don't worry
the fish are muddle-headed

Because of the danger
he wanted to see you
when he came back there was no more water in the ditch

Growing grapes   or
picking grapes   there are several
vineyards

    Holding her hand
    we walk toward the gate

        She's in the field
        she's also in the field
is that what is called "Safety First"?

47. West Market

Knife of the law is key to the court

The small dragon bed, murdered

48. Huokou Neighborhood

Snow covered me
in the tree
rubbing softly
        our hands
that was a night you too passed by

Snow under the lamplight dimly seen
from the farm
bringing three scarves   and three blankets
    never expecting
the impassable passage through the trees

Winter birds are trains
winter birds
I thought
        after two years

winter would be gone

She came
to lead me
        walking away   (she went in first)

Woods all around

-   Winter birds are trains •
-   winter birds are calling, calling •
-   don't winter birds get cold? •
          winter birds don't get cold
small • harvest

49. *Government Street*

Watching her for a while
        peeling bamboo shoots for a while
                better if a knife were a little longer

50. *Rostrum Road*

With each step of the Long March my longing
loses its way

51. *Hidden Moon Alley*

No one could get inflamed   busy lighting lamps
Zapitalism   flashes down into the depths

52. *Painted Foundation*

When you dream
don't say   the heartwood is spotless white
don't say   that you came last time
                 who is the wife
digging in the place where there are no dead

(Take note)
her smile   is a little sad
    shining   (looking after her home)
her mole   is a little sad
    yes, the reception desk

I haven't seen you for so long
don't really   bury
              your child
              this son of sadness
don't mark the mole on the hand of your adopted boy

Epilogue

BACK TO MY FAMILY[1]

I see your hands
shading your eyes from the sun's glare
I see your hair
falling from under your cap
smiling
I see the shadow cast by your hand
your cart stands off to one side
Sam
you wouldn't recognize me now
I have been gone so long

I left you
because I was afraid to look at you
my love
was like glass
and it was fear that made
you take my hand on the stairs
saying, "Hey, Chubs"
you wanted me to take you home

When you were sleeping
I saw your tears
you grasped white flowers in your hands
I spanked you
you said I was bad daddy
then you said, "But Chubs likes me"
you know all there is to know

Sam
you have no idea how I miss you now

---

1 This poem was written in an airplane September 3, 1993, and mailed from Gu Cheng's island on October
   8. Sam is the name of Gu Cheng's son; Chubs is Gu Cheng's nickname, which his son also called him.

177

separated by the sea
the sea hugs your little island
the trees on the island
nanny and your toys
how much I want to hug you
when the evening comes upon me

Sam
I want to tell you something
yes, Sam, I do like you
these words are only for you
no one else will hear
I love you, Sam
I want to go home
take me back home with you

You're so young
and already know
that I'll come back
to see you
to lift you slowly in the air
Sam, you're in the sun's glow
and so am I

Selected Prose

PREFACE TO *NAMELESS FLOWERS* (1976)

This collection of poems, *Nameless Flowers*, will be forever out of tune with the times. That's because it is a simple and honest account of the abnormal personality of a boy who was banished to the countryside with his father during the Cultural Revolution.

This boy (who was me in the past) wandered back and forth in the tidal flats of a vast and desolate coastline, never finding the font of wisdom, nor seeing the light of truth that he sought. Thus, little by little his natural stubbornness and sense of hope sank into the muddy pools of despondency. All that he could do at that point was to stoke the dying kitchen fires with wood from old coffins that the local peasants superstitiously avoided. Gradually he came to fear people, especially any "official" (because of the cold expression in their gazes). He was all alone, only able to commune with selfless nature; in this way he escaped from the turmoil of the human world.

Of course, after these times have slipped into the deep strata of history, the *Nameless Flowers* will themselves become merely lightly veined fossils of the modern. I cherish and preserve them now, not because I somehow hope to recover my lost youth, but rather because these will provide archaeologists of the future with some materials for their investigations. With these they will be able to prove that back in the 1960s and 1970s there was a bank of dark clouds over this barren piece of earth.

POETRY LESSONS (1980)

1.

It was a raindrop that first introduced me to poetry.

On the way to my primary school there was a spire-like pine tree, but whenever I passed by it never spoke.

Then one day, after a rain shower, when the world was fresh and clean, that pine tree suddenly was all aglitter, with crystalline raindrops hanging from every needle; at that moment I completely lost touch with my own being. Inside each single drop I saw a rainbow floating; each drop was full of the clear blue sky; each drop held a new world for me. . . .

I knew then that a single small drop of rain was able to contain everything, and to distill everything within it. The world that sparkled in the raindrop was purer and more beautiful than the world in which we live our lives.

Thus, a poem is just that: a raindrop glittering on some tree of the imagination.

2.

I grew up on a stretch of barren, alkaline land.

The earth and sky there were of a perfect beauty, they formed a perfect sphere. There were no hills, no trees; not even the angular lines of a building to disturb the view.

When I walked along my imaginary road, there was only me between the earth and sky: me, along with a type of pale purple plant.

These plants grew tall in that salty soil, so slender and dense; they stood beneath the sky, under dark clouds and blazing sun, accepting all that befell them. No one knew that they were there, no butterflies, no bees, there were no startled sighs or praises sung about them. Nonetheless, they grew, putting forth their small flowers, proudly holding their heads high. . . .

They taught me about springtime, poetry, and poetry's duty.

3.

Between the outcropping of coral headlands, there was a small sandy beach.

There in the sand, over many years, the tides had left behind shells, forever beautiful and undisturbed.

But when I stopped, what drew my attention were not those brightly colored shells, but rather a very plain spiral shell, one that scuttled there alone through the shallows. When I grabbed hold of it, I then realized that there was a crab hiding inside, alive.

I want to thank that crab for teaching me about poetic language.

One spirited spoken phrase, unique in its construction, is far better than dozens of antiquated and elegant expressions.

4.

Because of my deep needs, I often travel the far edges of society.

There, in front of me are plants, clouds, and the sea—nature cast in green, white and blue. The purity of these colors wipes away the dust of the everyday world, letting my mind recover its senses.

Is this something I am learning for the first time? No, it seems to be a recollection of an earlier time, as if before I was born I was one of them. I once was curved like the tusk of a mammoth, once as innocent as a leaf, once as minute and happy as floating plankton, that free . . .

I want to thank nature for letting me discover myself, discover the story of all things of the world, living and not. I want to thank it for giving me an endless supply of poems and songs.

This is why in the midst of the battle with reality, in the midst of the howl of the grinding machines, I still can still say in a sweet, quiet voice:

I'm yours.

5.

All things, material or alive, including people, have their dreams.

Each of these dreams is of its own world.

The desert dreams of the cloud's dark shadow, flowers dream of the butterfly's kiss; and dew dreams of the sea . . .

I too have a dream. Distant but distinct, it is not just of its own world, it is of a paradise beyond the world.

It is beautiful and pristine. When I opened the book of fairy tales by Hans Christian Andersen, my young mind flooded with light.

I travel toward it, gradually becoming transparent, casting away the shadow behind me. There is only the road, the open road.

The value of my life is in this moving on.

I want to use the pure metal of my mind to forge a key to open the gates of this paradise for people to see. If possible, I will then have the good fortune to sink into the darkness.

MISTY POETRY: AN INTERVIEW (1981)

Q: Recently we have been reading about different interpretations of the much discussed "misty poetry" (menglongshi). We were hoping you might answer some questions about this from your own point of view.

A: I'd be glad to do so.

Q. First, could you discuss what has been called "misty poetry," particularly what these poems may have in common.

A. This name "misty poetry" has a strong sense of Chineseness to it, and it's a term that came about in a quite conventional way. The name was actually first used several years ago, but at that time the type of poetry that the term now "represents" had just come into being and hadn't yet gone through its formal christening. Later, when people began to take notice of this new poetry, it had already suffered through a rough childhood and had become a rapidly growing teenager. But the question was, what would it be called?

Different people working from different perspectives came up with different names for it: new modern poetry, misty poetry, peculiar poetry, etc. Later, when the controversy erupted, we needed some commonly accepted terminology. What could we do? Our traditional way is to compromise; so "misty poetry" became the common expression.

My fellow poets and I have always thought that term "misty poetry" was a little misty itself. What does this word "misty" mean? According to its classical usage, it suggests a feeling something akin to "flowers viewed through the fog" or "losing sight of the ford crossing in the moonlight." According to the new theories, the term refers to poetry that is symbolic and suggestive, with deep conceptions, layered impressions, and a consciousness of the subconscious, etc. There's certainly some sense to this, but if you limit yourself to these ideas, I don't feel you'll really grasp the defining characteristic of this new sort of poetry. The defining characteristic of this new type of poetry is its realism—it begins with objective realism, but veers toward a subjective realism; it moves from a passive reaction toward active creation.

Basically, this poetry is not misty at all, but rather involves the awakening of a new type of aesthetic consciousness, whose field of concern is gradually becoming more clearly distinguished.

Q: You have said that "the defining characteristic" of "this new type of poetry" is that it "veers toward a subjective realism and moves toward active creation . . . whose field of concern is gradually becoming more clearly distinguished." But there are others who claim that the defining characteristic of these poems is that they are difficult to understand. What do you think of this "difficulty in understanding" the poetry?

A: In slightly more scholarly terms, "to understand" means "to comprehend." I don't believe that it has ever been a simple matter to comprehend poetry or humanity. Comprehension always depends on two points of view, that of the writer and that of the reader. These two points of view are determined by many factors; among the most important are: 1) the stage of one's aesthetic development, 2) one's lived experience, 3) one's personality, and 4) the success of the writer to capture the moment.

Let's first talk about stages of aesthetic development. Anyone who has even a rudimentary understanding of critical theory knows that aesthetic judgments are not cast in stone, but rather are constantly evolving with broad social change and one's individual development. If we speak of social change, then this is like the flow of a river; if we speak of the individual development, it is like the growth of a tree.

Back when I was reading only comic books, I once flipped through something by Walt Whitman. I was shocked. Was he some sort of nut? His language was completely goofy; how could this ever get published? Was the publisher nuts too? Didn't his mom know how to bring him up right? It was all so scary. But there were lots of scary things back then: for example, there were also Lu Xun and Qu Yuan! Luckily they were all a lot older than me and it wasn't anything for me to worry about, so I went back to my comic books.

Of course, later I gradually came to comprehend such literature: from the children's tale "The Song of the Stream" by Yan Wenjing (1956) to the short story "Long Flowing Water" by Liu Zhen (1960s), from O. Henry to Jack London, to Hugo, to Romain Rolland, to Tagore, etc. And when I reread Qu Yuan's "Encountering Sorrow" or Whitman's *Leaves of Grass* I was shocked, but shocked in a very different way than when I was young. This was a shock of being overwhelmed by the work.

When I asked my fellow poets about this, it turned out it was the same for them. At any given moment of their lives, in each stage of their aesthetic development, every one of them had works of which they were especially fond. This fondness was something that evolved, however, and the final objects of their attention were always those works most widely appreciated by humanity. Moreover, these works (except for children's literature) could not be comprehended by someone in primary school. This is a normal phenomenon.

In addition to "not understanding" because of one's stage of aesthetic development, a lack of comprehension can also be caused by different artistic styles and different conceptions of art. Some of these disparities normally co-occur, but sometimes distortions result from the sense of practicality that is the legacy of our "time of turmoil." If we weigh these distorted ideas against our traditional Chinese aesthetics, we cannot say they are normal.

During the time of the "Gang of Four" people became used to viewing the literary arts as mere explications of government policy printed in an attractive format, as if literature were a "multiform system" for fighting illiteracy. And poetry? It became merely a competition of rhyming editorials. Later, things got somewhat better; starting with the "April Fifth Demonstrations" in 1976, poetry began to speak truthfully and show some hope of revival and development. Very quickly, as it began to reflect contemporary issues, this new poetry established some independent social value; this was very exciting for us. But was that all there was to be? Humankind needs other intellectual and emotional fields of interest. It is in these fields that our ancestors planted and harvested their art, and the fruits of their labors have become the stars that eternally shine in the sky of humanity. In recent years, however, these have largely become desolate lands filled with weeds. The fields of interest that are important to humankind include: the life of the mind, the wonder of nature, and those mysterious realms of which men can have no clear conception.

Such interests must be rediscovered and expanded; the vitality of the Chinese people must find expression, only then will there be those who go forth to explore new lands. These explorers will revere the master poets of ancient times, but they will not try to repeat the literary methods of the past; to repeat the old is not what art is about. These explorers will use their creative powers to express the needs and ideals of the new generation. (The so-called "misty poetry" is just one of these methods of expression.)

The conceptual reach of poetry finds so many forms and is so fecund that no one can encompass it with just one idea. Poetry's inherently dream-like quality determines that it will forever be opening new fields of interest, constructing new spiritual worlds. The philosophy of an unchanging response to the myriad changes will in the end become history.

In addition to the conceptual issues discussed above, there are also some things that pertain directly to the individual that should be considered since these have a clear role in the way poetry will resonate with someone. These are an individual's personality and life experience. These two factors determine, to a great degree, a person's specific connection to poetry. Since personality is a very difficult thing to assess, I will skip that and speak only of the role of one's life experience.

We have received many letters from young readers that raise such issues. Why is it that it is mostly young people who like "misty poetry"? How is it that the hearts of these really not very well-read young people can find a way to beat together in the distant world of "misty poetry"? Is this some purely surrealistic condition? No, it is not! What is important is that this younger generation has shared a journey together, has faced a shared reality, and has searched for ideals together.

Of course, those who seek the truth must pay the price; when you try to cut a new path though the wilds, you will encounter more thorns than flowers. Life is like that, and so is the creative learning process of the writer—more thorns than flowers. Both age and things unknown will mean that there will always be failures, going the long way around, running aground, hitting snags, maybe even sinking forever into oblivion. There is no glory to speak of in this. Ordinary people will think these artists are silly, and relatives and friends will be distressed for them. Yet, a nation needs people who will first sacrifice themselves, because among them there will be some who are able to learn from the failures of their companions and find a new direction, in the end discovering new lands and new horizons.

Q: Your analysis above regarding the issue of "understanding" literature has given us some insight into the controversy surrounding "misty poetry." Since you do not agree with "this sort of narrow function of poetry and the literary arts," what do you think the social function of poetry and the literary arts should be?

A: I have said that poetry with its conceptual reach finds many forms, and thus I think social function also has many forms. I appreciate politically engaged poetry that directly exposes social problems, and I like even more lyrical poetry that gives creative expression to the beauty of the spiritual and natural worlds. I believe all truly beautiful poetry has some positive social value. The sword and the rose do not stand opposed, to fight is not our purpose, the fight is just a means by which we can improve the world. From this point of view, the sword is there for the rose.

Having paid such a great price, we now know that neither politics nor material objects can be all there is to life. If a people are to move forward, they need more than technology and science, they also need higher spiritual cultivation, including a new form of aesthetic consciousness. Beauty cannot be held prisoner or enslaved any longer. It must be like the sun and the moon, filled with light, rising high into the sky, chasing away the shadows of evil; it will then fall through the windows of art and poetry to shine on souls of people both awakened and sound asleep.

For the next generation to rise above us, we now need more, cleaner, and larger windows.

WITH A TV MOUNTED ON THE WALL   (1983)

1.

When he heard the knock on the door, Tom walked casually over and opened it.

The two visitors were both strangers, one tall and one short, dressed in green clothes that glowed in the dark.

"Can I help you?" asked Tom.

Without a word or change in their expressions the two walked right past Tom, went through the living room, stepping over the chairs, and very calmly entered his bedroom. There they fell onto the bed, apparently not caring that the quilt was disgustingly dirty and rumpled.

"Excuse me? Who are you looking for? What the hell do you think you are doing? You . . . "

The one who was somewhat taller (no, actually he was really quite tall) began to undo his shoe laces; suddenly he looked over at Tom and said, "We're not looking for anyone, we live here."

Tom was dumbfounded by what these first-rate jerks had just done. After about half a minute he found his voice, and said in a serious tone, "Excuse me, sirs, but this is my home. Now please leave!"

"I won't disagree with that," the shorter one replied softly, then, patting the pillow a few times, fell asleep.

Tom became so upset that he pounded on the bedstead, swearing and cursing them, "You bastards, you jerks!"; then he yanked the quilt off of them and tossed it across the room. But what good did that do? None. The visitors just lay there, sleeping even more soundly, their hairy legs stuck out stiffly across the bed; they even began to drool some.

With a scream, Tom picked up a folding chair, but just as he was about to hurl it at them, he suddenly caught himself. He thought, "I could have killed them."

Nervously, with his fist in his mouth, Tom circled round and round, trying to use his somewhat shaky reasoning to figure out what was going on. Drunk? Or crazy? Yes, that's it, they must be crazy! They are some crazies let out of the insane asylum for a holiday. I need to make a call!

But the phone was busy, and it was still busy when he tried again. The snoring behind him was getting louder. Tom thought he might be going crazy himself, so repressing the urge to scream, he grabbed his coat and ran out into the street.

2.

Ghosts! Everywhere the street glowed green, even the granite posts of the streetlights, which were covered with moss. Phone booths had either disappeared, or were filled with people. The doorway to the police station was so crowded not even light could get through. What was going on? Tom spotted a public notice coming in and out of view between the heads bobbing in front of him:

SERIOUS PUBLIC NOTICE

This station accepts only cases involving bodily harm or the loss of private property. For example: nosebleeds, middle fingers cut on broken glass, trousers burned or smoke-damaged, flower vases placed on the wrong window sills, old-fashioned fountain pens brought home filled with ink from the office, not paying cash for atomic bombs, etc.

If a case falls outside the scope of these conditions—such a dispute arising because two people are sleeping in someone's house—this station must not only disregard the case, but must also levy a fine . . . .

Oh, mother! As Tom stood there reading, he felt as if he were sinking into a trap. He felt as if he was going to slip under the people pressed around him, slip into the ground and become . . . Fortunately before he sank all the way down, he saw another part of the notice:

> . . . *if this sort of dispute has actually occurred, then the person can take exception and go to the courthouse and see Superior Court Judge Yah Sue; he will inform you on how to proceed . . .*

3.

When Tom pushed open the door to the courthouse, he found Superior Court Judge Yah Sue just then adding some sugar to his coffee. The Judge received Tom in a very friendly sort of way, shaking his hand, patting him on the shoulder, and asking him if he wanted something to drink. Then he listened to Tom's entire accusation, which Tom told on the verge of tears.

When the Judge had listened to the whole story, he began to ponder the issues. As he pondered, he blew on his coffee, which was already stone cold. When he was done, he just shrugged and said to Tom:

"Mr. Tom, sir, I am very sympathetic to your situation, but there is nothing I myself can do. Your case is a housing dispute, this court does not accept such cases, it hasn't for quite some time now."

"Then what sort of cases do you accept?"

"That we decide according to our needs," said the Judge in a seemingly proper sort of way.

"Your needs?" Tom was taken back for a second, his head pounded like it was about to explode. "Then, where are cases such as mine accepted?"

"Actually, I don't think they are accepted anywhere."

"What?"

"You still don't understand, do you? As cases of this sort become more and more common, it is harder and harder to get them heard, and moreover . . . ."

Still don't understand? Tom was so mad he was just about to start stomping around in some sort of Hindu dance right there on the courthouse floor. But he controlled himself, and asked, "If I were to smash a chair over the heads of those two fellows, then what would happen?"

"That'd be a case of personal assault with bodily harm. The police would deal with that, and we'd hear the case here."

Tom was now exhausted from the waves of anger passing over him. He just stood there tapping lightly on the chair with his thick knuckles. Finally he sighed and quite unexpectedly said, "Would Your Honor mind telling me where you live?"

He then realized that the Judge might be startled by this, so he laughed heartily and said, "I'd just like for us to become friends."

It was indeed strange. But the Judge didn't think much of it; he just snapped his fingers like some kid, took out an elegant name card and placed it in Tom's hand.

4.

121 Ocean Avenue was not bad at all—a nice-looking apartment building. As he slipped in through the revolving door, Tom couldn't help but laugh to himself, "Well, Your Honor, what about a housing dispute of your own? You won't be able to hear that case either?"

Tom walked along the deep purple carpet, smiling coldly. He did not notice that the attendants in the building seemed somehow familiar, their clothes all appearing to have a greenish cast. This was especially so for the one beside the elevator. And what was that look on his face when he saw the name card? And why the push from behind?

The elevator rose by fits and starts, springy underneath his feet. Tom suddenly thought: he wouldn't have a wife, would he? Would she be a little plum of a thing, or an old prune? If there's a wife, what should I say? And, oh my god, what if by chance there's a little rugrat? Children are completely blameless. Tom suddenly hated himself. Why hadn't *he* gotten married? If he had had a wife, he probably could've avoided having those jerks in his house.

Just as he was hesitating, about to beat a hasty retreat, the elevator door opened. "You have arrived," said the loudspeaker. Tom gave a shudder, and then involuntarily walked out into the room.

How strange. What kind of room was this? Empty, with wire mesh over all the tall, narrow windows. "Clang," the door with iron bars closed tightly behind him. Very secure, he thought, just like a prison.

After ten minutes of staring into space, Tom began to shiver. He realized this really was a prison. He couldn't call out, there would be no response, it seemed that everything outside had disappeared.

There was only one thing in his prison cell. A TV screen was mounted high on the wall, indestructible, about the size of a book.

Its blue screen flickered, day and night, with the same caption, "Think! If you want complete understanding."

Yes, think. Tom held his head in his hands, squatting down, and thought for many years; up until yesterday, he still had not understood.

POETRY AND LIFE (1985)

Reading books offers one enlightenment.

Yet when Adam and Eve, in their state of innocence, discovered the meaning of good and evil, paradise was lost.

And when Master Wonton, with his blissful disposition, got his seven orifices bored into his pristine body, he fell apart and died.

For me, living singularly and unlike others, is the most important form of enlightenment.

Gazing out from the palm of the hand, the fires have already died out. The girls are moving like pasture grasses, and the boys are sending out their beams of light. Among the minerals and the flowing waters, trees one by one enter deep into the earth, their green roots exposed to the open air.

I once experienced complete destruction, when the earth raised up its feet so that beneath them the sky shone brightly. The woman crossing through the square, her transparent blue skirt fluttering around her legs, did not believe.

Scholars everywhere lifted their gaze, and behind them instruments and windows flashed and glittered; they did not believe either. All the others, and those who were making a racket beside the pots and pans, lifted their gaze.

The destruction is no more, and I have already traveled through life a thousand times before. Now I walk along a small boy's wretched road.

I place them, those peals of laughter, on top of the fence.

I have already traveled through life a thousand times before. Before, there were ferns and plowshares on the hillside, but books had not yet been born; and words, thin and tiny, still crawled through the mud; nor had medieval towers yet been raised up.

A ladybug crawls in the dew, sleeping, waking, sleeping and waking; blinking slowly, it does not dream. At the edge of the sky, the pale purple color of a rainbow shines.

Sleeping mushroom; waking ladybug. One by one approaching, then running away, to form a thousand lotus blossoms, in this world fingers are drawn into fist. It likes to play games with itself like this.

EATING AT DESERT CREEK (1992)

It was the summer of 1985. Beijing had organized a group of writers to travel to Heilongjiang Province to give encouragement to some of the educated youth who had been left behind there after the Cultural Revolution. General

189

Secretary Hu Yaobang made the appeal, and the Beijing Labor Bureau funded the trip. I went as a representative of the Beijing Writer's Union. But actually, there was no work. Once we got on the train, all of us began to shoot the breeze like old buddies. I was laughing away too. I had brought along some yeast cakes and witch-hazel pills for my indigestion since I was planning to eat it up with the others; this was a rare opportunity.

As soon as we got to Desert Creek, then the eating really began in earnest. Everyone got a meal card with his name and number on it, and we worked our way in a snaking line into the dining room of the guest house. An eight-course meal, plus soup. Although it was just a small rural unit, they had prepared sea cucumber, shark's fin, prawns, and even a type of golden pheasant from Jiulongkou that had been enjoyed by the Qian Long Emperor of the Qing Dynasty. At first I thought this was because it was our reception dinner, but it turned out every day was like this. And the help also delivered fruit and snacks to our rooms. We guests from on high were treated not just as deities descending to earth, but even as the Kitchen God returning to his palace in heaven.

In those days, I was making a special effort to take care of the more spiritual side of my life, so after I had eaten my fill, I thought I would go out for a stroll. The sky was just beginning to darken; outside the building there was a police car. When I went out the gate I saw people looking about in the dark with flashlights. In the dim light I could make out ten or twenty cops, with their sleeves rolled up; I didn't pay them much attention. Once I got out to the road, with the evening darkness beginning to set it, there were policemen at the intersections checking out the passing vehicles with their flashlights. There were no pedestrians on the road, which couldn't help but make me suspicious, so I took off my name card and put it away in my pocket. I thought I might go along sort of incognito, but suddenly a beam of light fell on me, and I was grabbed from behind.

"What the hell are you doing?"

"I, I . . . " I really didn't how to explain what I was doing, so I just said, "From Beijing."

"Let's see your ID."

"I didn't bring it with me," I said in a panic. Then I took out my meal card, upon which was written, "Beijing Writers Union, No. 8, Gu Cheng." After the guy looked it over, he let me go, telling me to watch out for the mosquitoes. Naturally I was afraid of mosquitoes, but the truth is I was more afraid of the cops. Having regained my freedom, I returned to the guest house. Nearing the building, I discovered that there were flashlights moving about everywhere; it seemed like some sort of encirclement.

When I got back to my room, I quickly told the other guys about the alert that was going on outside; I suspected they were looking for an assassin or something. But one of the other writers, who now had his sights set on writing the great Marxist novel and earlier had worked for the Desert Creek Brigade, said he didn't think that was the case. "No, it's always like that around here." He said that during the day when he was visiting Number Three Farm, the people in the security office there told him that there was someone who was planning to lodge a complaint with the authorities, so they'd rounded up all the likely suspects and locked them away in some undisclosed location.

"Really?" One guy frowned, another slapped the bed.

"That's really terrible." Some one else said that people from here need-ed to have a letter of permission to buy a train ticket. But Old Chen from the Writers Union didn't believe it. "But didn't it look pretty good when we went to look things over today? Every family had a TV, a cow . . . "

"But those were just recently distributed. Authorities in Tianjin sent the funds; then the farm lent the stuff to the peasants so they can make a movie— 300 for the TV, 9,000 for the cow."

"But didn't Tianjian provide the funding?"

"Yes, they gave the money to the farm, but these were loans to the peas-ants."

"If you don't believe it, just ask tomorrow . . ."

"One family's cow died; now they're completely distraught because they'll never be able to repay the loan . . ."

The next day the visit went as expected. Although it was a tiny village, it was festooned with colorful banners; there was even a group of twenty or thirty children with rouged cheeks to provide the requisite "warm welcome." We were taken to look at the cows, pigs, and little black-and-white TVs in five homes. I started off on my own toward a sixth place when our guide got all in a panic, telling me that I shouldn't go wandering around. When I kept on going, he pulled me aside and told me they would be punished if I wan-dered off, so I stopped right there. All I could do was to observe those piti-ful "homes of model families." In every one they brought out the same candy and cigarettes; on the walls hung photos of the residents as Brigade Soldiers and Educated Youth: driving a large cart, sporting a red flower, in their pre-tend dance across the desolate land, the boy's hair neatly parted; and the girl's done in thick braids. The caption read, "With One Shove of the Spade, She Establishes a New Village."

"Did you build this house yourselves?"

"Yes, but now it's owned by the cadre office of the farm. If they want to sell it, they could get about 2,000 for it."

"How much do you make a year?"

"We make whatever we make, but no matter what, we always owe them 2,000."

"How can you owe them money?"

"Well, in addition to the taxes, there's also their management fee—280 per person. When the harvest is good, we owe 2,000; when the harvest is bad, we owe even more. And we can never leave; we only hope to send our children back to the city to study . . ."

Although this was the oldest trick in the book—fooling the leaders but not the followers—when I got back to the guest house I was still upset. That afternoon I didn't feel like going out again. Old Chen from the Writers Union was in a difficult spot himself (in his pocket he had two letters of petition that he'd been asked to pass on to the central authorities); he reprimanded me, saying that I had to go. Later when we were discussing the "Grand Circumstances" of which Mao spoke, one of the abandoned educated youth who was serving as a nurse in the brigade snorted and blurted out, "I'd be glad to switch places with whoever thinks this place is so 'grand' We're willing to go back to the city to shovel shit." All the leaders sat there with a pained smile on their lips—even the work of the revolution seemed to need a division of labor.

Things being the way they were, it was even hard to eat; only watermelon would go down. Thus, we held on until the last day. That evening we were to have a get-together. In preparation for the poetry reading, the leader of the Beijing poetry-reading troupe was walking in the hallway, flushed in the face, getting ready with yoga breathing exercises. "To have a child, a child called Explorer." I don't know if he had any children or not. I did know that just before this trip he had raised a pile of money for the troupe, which he owned, by presenting a poem to some tycoon in Hong Kong. Now, during this trip he was standing there among the younger, politically connected kids in our group, and he actually did not look too bad, except, of course, for his lack of hair. Clearly someone who has risen to such heights, deserved his three meals a day; as for myself, I was too ashamed to eat at all.

I lay on my bed with my "stomach ache," waiting for the time to pass. Good-hearted Chen came by again to see how I was doing. Old Chen really did have a good heart: he got all worried just watching a child cross the street; and was shocked by any sort of untoward behavior; he'd cry out in a strained voice, "How can anyone be like that?" On this trip he had been using funds allocated by the Labor Bureau to pay all the bills. Fearing an outbreak of the flu, he even bought us a supply of vitamin C, which we swallowed ten pills at time—actually this was most useful for combating the effects of eating too much greasy food. Chen was still concerned that I wasn't feeling well; the leadership had suggested that no doubt I could steel myself and read a poem since my head was still fine. I said that he could choose stomach ache or headache, but I could only think of one line of poetry, and that wasn't very noteworthy: "To have a child, a child called Exploited."

COPPER (1992)

Traveling through Heilongjiang Province still, we left the large tour group and set out on our own toward Harbin. It was like being a real poet—on the road with a group of editors from *The Poet* magazine. We swaggered through the streets, bullshitting with each other and looking for a bathroom. As we walked along the street, I spotted something on the ground, leaned down, picked it up and put in my pocket. All my brother poets were curious about what I'd found. I showed it to them; it was a piece of electrical wire. What are you going to do with that? They stood there on the side of the road gazing out across the waves of incoming poetry—I told them it was made of copper.

I am crazy about copper of all kinds: red copper, brass, copper nickel alloy, bronze. I have been collecting it since I was small, never walking past a single piece. In the beginning, obviously it was for the money: 1.5-2 RMB per catty, depending on the quality. I once sold a brass lock for 47 cents; that made a great impression on me. But no one bought copper wire or electrical cable, figuring that copper used by industry was part of the national resources. I did not understand why they wouldn't buy brass keys since they bought locks. Could it be that keys were private property, but locks were not?

I loved copper because I had experienced a vision. The luster of copper is beautiful, especially when in its molten state. One time at home we had a large brass belt buckle that had broken, and we had it melted down. Seeing the luster of that molten copper made me want to own my own welding torch when I grew up. The melting point of copper is 1,000 degrees, so for some-one like me who was melting pieces of lead on the cooking stove, that was like a glowing dream. In order to have enough copper someday to realize my dream, I started collecting it, sometimes spending hours just freeing up a brass screw. Once in the paper I read about some thrifty fanatic who saved up 4,000 catties of copper wire ends which he gave to the state. This really got me excited; so when I was in fourth grade I spent half a semester digging copper tubing out of abandoned toilets. My mind was filled with the bril-liance of flowing copper.

My desire for copper brought me to discover a copper mine in a pile of coal. Smelting copper this way was my own invention. I would take chunks of copper sulfide and place them in an iron wok and heat them up until red. The sulfur would burn off in a blue flame; after the flame burned out, a thin layer of copper would remain on the surface of the wok. This is what I think is called "reduction." Smelting this way could yield only copper powder, yet still I dreamed of casting my own copper coins and brass swords; I dreamed of opening a bank that would issue its own copper currency.

If you like something too much it can become a perversity. From copper, I came to like numismatics, metallurgy, casting, molding, copper statuary, bronze vessels, sulfur, gunpowder, brass cannons, bronze beetles, and entomological classification . . . The first time Bei Dao came back from Scandinavia, he brought back a little brass cannon as a gift for me, his tight-fisted friend. Later when I was leaving the country, I gave it to someone else.

There were so many things that I wanted to cast. I prepared a crucible and molds for swords, and I had two boxes of copper saved. This was the copper I had collected from Beijing to Shandong, from Shandong to Shanghai, and from Shanghai back to the city of Beijing. With plans to make castings, I also prepared a furnace and electric fan; these were set up in the small courtyard of a friend of mine. I was so covetous of a boiler-room electric blower, I couldn't help but look for employment as a boiler worker in a power plant—all just for the flow of some molten copper.

But I left China and was separated far from my copper.

When my mother was moving her house, she wrote and asked me what to do with the copper. Sell it, I said, as long as you can get 2 RMB a catty.

There's just so much copper in the trash of these foreign countries.

YING'ER[1] (1993)

It is hardly out of the ordinary for a poet to have a lover. Everyone who writes poetry has affairs, sometimes secretly, sometimes not. It's just all too common. But I've never heard of someone actually having two wives; that would hardly be very romantic, so I don't think that it is really possible. (p. 47)

* * *

When I finally found the house for sale in the classifieds, I took the small ad over to show to my professor friend. At first glance, he suspected the house was a strange sort of place. So we took a boat across the bay to take a look at it. The house was in the dense woods, high in the hills; inside we found a person sitting there, attentively at work on crafting jewelry out of

---

1 These selections have been rearranged to give a more coherent sense of that essential story of love, lust, and disappointment from Gu Cheng's autobiographical novel *Ying'er*. The novel recounts, in language of reflection and fantasy, the story of Gu Cheng, his wife (Lei), and lover (Ying'er), and was finished in the final months of his life. Citations refer to the 1993 Yuanshen (Taiwan) edition.

seashells. When we walked across the rickety boards into the house, he raised his head and said to us, "The end of the world is near."

"About how much time do we have left?" I asked him.

He said, "Probably another fifty years or so."

"That's plenty of time," I said. "I need only twenty years."

He took us for a walk along a dark and damp path, up to the top of the hill where there was another small cabin. Opening the door, I could see straight out to the sea. I knew then this was the place I had been looking for.

When we left Auckland we had a bonfire that lasted all night, we burnt all the things that we didn't need. We brought only some biscuits and vegetable seedlings with us to the island.

Lei wrapped the baby in a small blanket and placed him on the only sofa we had, and then she got down to work. That night was filled with wind and rain and we lit a candle. I looked at Lei and said, "This is the place I have been looking for for twenty years. I've been looking for it ever since I left school when I was twelve." That night the wind and rain were so heavy that they shook the little house; outside a tree as big around as a barrel was blown over.

Whenever the wind blew like that, the ocean was covered with spewing foam and towering waves, and the university would call and ask if the ferry were running and whether I'd be able to come in.

Whenever I was not at the university, I busied myself gathering firewood from the forested hills. Since we had no electricity, that meant we cooked, heated water, and dried diapers all by the wood fire. Inside the house could be very cold, so we had to start a fire to drive away some of the dampness. After three days of heavy rain, Lei went out, promising to gather a lot of firewood.

After taking care of the baby, she'd drag the heavy branches of fallen trees down the mountain.

Our one neighbor became a very good friend. On Sundays he would take us to the country market, but we couldn't afford to buy anything. On the way, Lei would be forever pointing out this and that, asking if any of these plants could be eaten or not. Once he said something to the effect that a certain tropical palm could be eaten. Lei ran back to tell me, "You can eat this tree." I chopped down that huge tree and started tasting everything on it, from the twigs to roots; the seeds looked sort of like corn. Lei had prepared a fire and waited for me to bring something home. But she had wasted her time, for I didn't find anything on that tree that was edible. Only later did we discover that it was the stems of the flowers that could be eaten; they were something like bamboo shoots.

Another time all we had to eat were wild leeks.

At the university Julia called me, saying, "Your wife is on the phone."

I ran over to get the call, the voice on the phone was very weak. Lei said that she had fallen down the stairs and everything was out of focus. It turns out she was poisoned from eating too many wild leeks; when she was going downstairs to get water from the cistern, she had collapsed.

When I got off work in the evening, Lei would humor the baby to sleep, and come through the woods to meet me at the bus stop.

Slowly we were actually able to start getting by, finding the firewood and food we needed, and slowly fixing up our home. At that time I wrote a letter to Ying'er and told her that I felt like building a wall to keep the world out. And it seems as if Ying'er were also very world-weary, so tired it seemed she would die. This made me upset. Little by little, I ate less to save some money. I wanted to have her come right away. Then things in Beijing turned for the worse, and I was afraid something might happen to her.

. . .

I had dreamed about it so often, and then finally she got her passport. On the telephone I listened to her speak softly about getting the passport, the fights, the visa. Her voice seemed different. I looked at Lei; she seemed somewhat hesitant, but then quickly agreed to buy the airplane ticket.

In her letter to me, Ying'er wrote that she did not want to speak in a loud voice, she wanted to let the leaves on the trees return. With a charcoal pencil she had sketched our island and its bay, the tropical palms, and the new home of her imagination.

Ying'er really came. (pp. 419–21)

* * *

The first time we did it was when we were living in Shady Valley. That afternoon we were at Elizabeth's house, all standing around in her big living room. You left us there to ourselves, to return in a while.

Ying'er didn't know what she should do. A new place, with pebbles below the eaves and dried flowers in the tall ceramic vase. In my growing desire, I took her gently into my arms. She moved with me over onto the sofa; there are always new feelings in a new place. I slowly unbuttoned her blouse; she calmly said, "Lei will return in a little while, we should go into the back."

A little while later, we were still there in that sunny bedroom when we heard your car drive up. But we were finished. Feeling content, I stood off to one side of the room and watched her throw her clothes back on, then return to the table in the living room.

You walked in, bringing Little Chubs with you.

It was there that her sense of reserve, as if she had been raped, disappeared. Elizabeth's house really changed her. It was a big house, with no one around, just the shadows of the bamboo moving in the wind. There was a wood-burning cast-iron stove, and two bedrooms. That's where we spent our first night together.

She was sitting on the edge of the bed after her bath and I watched her take off her pale purple bathrobe. Then I reached out with my hand to touch her. I caressed her clean; glowing skin, caressed her breasts; I was suddenly moved by a feeling, both mysterious and common. She and I were together, and the pleasure we felt slowly mounted.

When our bodies touched together, skin on skin, I learned how stirred she was, and what gave her pleasure.

I took a condom out of a little box, and she asked softly, "Are you going to use that?" I fussed with it for a bit, but I was embarrassed to admit that I'd never used one before. She laughed and said. "You don't even know how to do that!"

It sounded like she really knew what she was talking about. She gave me some instructions, "Like this, unroll it like this." But actually she didn't know how to use one either. Then she suddenly realized this was not her responsibility.

With the rise and fall of our bodies, I found out how bold she could be, despite her usual timidity. She wanted me natural, unrestrained and wild, pounding like the waves of the foaming sea that try to make boats founder; she wanted me like the tall mast standing tightly wound in the blowing wind. We first sunk into that deep dark valley, then we climbed peaks in the sunset. We made love without speaking, never being afraid. Only then did I know how good we were together.

All I had to do was thrust a little, and she would cry out in pleasure. (pp. 81–82)

* * *

BLACK CAT

"She looks rather fetching."

When I saw the photograph that she had sent, I had immediately remembered what she was like. The gentle way she would come through the door; now she was standing there so nonchalantly in a well-tended orchard somewhere in South America.

"Do you want her now? Do you?" In the deep of the night Ying'er was tormenting me, whispering in my ear, "She stayed over with you. Did you do it with her then?"

"No."

"You didn't want her?" "I know you wanted her." (She got up to move about. In the morning she fixed her hair before going out.)

"Huh?"

"Why wouldn't you want her? Are you getting up now." (It was raining, and I was too sleepy to go back). The flashes of lightning crashed in the green poplar trees. "This lightning is too much, let's get up and eat a can of those peaches." (The lights that were on all dimmed a little. She spoke excitedly.)

"Then how about having me, just the way you wanted to do it with her? Would you like that?" Ying'er was talking faster and faster now; I could hear water lapping near my ears. The columns of water swirled and tumbled; the hot water pipes were covered in white; what could she see in that foggy mirror?

Ying'er stood naked on the stool, behind the table at the other side of the room. The light reflected off her plump legs, and off the dark patch in the crease between them. She looked at me defiantly. Having gotten away from me as I chased her, she stood leaning on the square pillar.

"If you don't let me get dressed, then I won't, I'll just stay like this. When Lei comes home, I'll just say it was you who took off my clothes. . . . When you see a woman coming out of the bathroom, do you imagine what she looks like without any clothes on? . . . You close your eyes. Haven't you seen a woman like this before?"

I asked, "When did you learn about it?"

"After I went to college."

"Before then you didn't have any ideas about it?"

"No, not really. I just knew that there was something to be afraid of. When you men do something bad, you don't even know it. I did ask an older girl from our neighborhood; at least at that time I thought she was older. 'So what is it, anyway?' She said, 'To sleep with someone.' 'Sleep?' I didn't understand at all. She just looked at me and went inside."

(Small, narrow footprints were visible in the sand. One by one, they appeared in a place where there were no people. They crossed the creek, its fallen bank, and then on down. They had come out from the sea.

He was an eight-year-old boy, his small naked penis coated with sand. He was looking for his lost shoe, carrying the other one in his hand. He and his trail of footprints were the only things on the beach.

He seemed to be able to see the lost shoe hanging, swinging in the air.

2 Wenxin, a writer and photographer from Beijing, met Gu Cheng, his wife Xie Ye (Lei), and his lover Li Ying (Ying'er) in the 1980s, and remained their friend and confidante until the end. This is Gu Cheng's last letter to her.

He did not know why that shoe would have left him, left the earth, and would be floating in some invisible lake.

He walked on, crossing reefs, and crossing streams.

The tidal pools trapped by the sand dunes were as cool as a mirror. The strings of algae in them were pale green; the transparent shrimp became visible only when they swam over the top of the algae. In the sand, clumps of grass grew every which way.

After he climbed to the top of the dunes, he could see the stand of willows beyond. Their branches had never been pruned and hung down to the ground; when the wind blew, they would brush across the sand. Among the branches floated several skirts.

He saw her.

She came out from the sea, tall and gorgeous, softly singing a song. In the morning light her hair fell loose, then was pulled back. Her pristine and porcelain body was exposed, along with that secret place, to the morning light. She first combed her hair, then let it fall; she raised up her arms and brought the bird songs to a halt.

After a long while she heard faint, sobbing sounds. Those were the sound of pale cicadas in the willow trees shedding their skins, repeating her song. She walked over, the boy was gone; there was a small tree growing out of his one shoe.)

Ying'er and I had thought of how we would write some stories together; even the book title had been chosen—either *Black Cat* or *At Fifteen*. We planned to write about her experiences of being a woman and the budding of desire, along with my strange fantasies. We wanted this book to describe our mutual desire in a simple and shared way. She was startled by my initial uncontrollable excitement; she shared with me each of my dreams, experiencing the danger in them. She let me stalk her like a black cat, or, when no one was around, to walk through her clothes drying in the sun. In the deep night, with the light beside her bed, I climbed a tree in full leaf, a chimney; there she let me walk about silently on her roof, or to fill the deserted room with drawings.

At fifteen: she liked this number, and how pretty she was then. She wondered at what point in our lives were we the closest: unknown to us in our shared destiny. At seventeen, she imagined that I would have been there on the street savagely sawing lumber, and she, carrying her book bag and wearing a flowered dress, would have quietly and absentmindedly walked by.

"I was too young," she said. "I was too young to meet you then. You were crazy." She knew that the street where I sawed lumber was only a few bus stops away from her school.

"Too young." When she came to know of my lust, she said, "How could I have known you were like this."

This is the book that never ever began. (pp. 266–270)

* * *

There are many things I can't tell you, words that you will never hear. I have talked to Lei about some of them. She knows how I miss you every day.

Ying'er, you can go on playing in the water, while I drown. The day we first met was indeed a lovely day.

I never expected this.

I never saw the two stairways you unveiled. Please, please come back and live with us. I enjoy seeing you together with Lei, even more than with me. I am nothing. You know that.

Should I end here? Since you are so timid, I'll be the good guy here.

It's over. (p. 54)

LAST LETTERS (1993)

Dear Wenxin,[2]

I am always starting letters to you but not finishing them, or not sending them. This time I promise, no matter what, I will send you these few pages tomorrow. Reading your letters makes me feel that our little kingdom has not been completely destroyed, that I am not completely without a home to which to return.

We are always talking about you. Perhaps you don't believe that but it is true. And I wrote you several letters that I never sent. I didn't send them because you're just too perfect, so emotionally charged; if someone is too perfect then others feel unworthy, knowing there's no way to measure up. Ying'er liked to do things with you because you always had "a way." She wasn't bothered by it at all. A half hour after she got up she became upset, but she said that she was just tired; that probably accounts for her coldness. As for me, I am ashamed of myself. Those mental problems of mine have now passed. But, Wenxin, I am like a dead person, there is nothing else left. Having the opportunity to pour over your letters is wonderful. Everyone else has closed the door on me, as I so deserve.

All the letters that I wrote to Ying'er are now in a desk at her home in Beijing. I can never get them back now. I don't care anymore, but those are my letters, not hers.

---

2 Wenxin, a writer and photographer from Beijing, met Gu Cheng, his wife Xie Ye (Lei), and his lover Li Ying (Ying'er) in the 1980s, and remained their friend and confidante until the end. This is Gu Cheng's last letter to her.

You have forgiven us, even though we were like shards of glass stabbing into others. You're a good person, not capable of hate. I'm the base one, and I am now very aware of my own nature. When you read my book [Ying'er] you will know how completely sick I am, only my hands are normal. I have scattered pieces of our ruined garden everywhere, scattered pieces of myself everywhere. See how the world has meant so little to me, but so much to her. I want to preserve those times together in that white cottage; she abandoned it, and so did I. The cottage did me harm. I shouldn't have left Beijing in the first place; I shouldn't have lived so long. The most beautiful days should be those just before the end.

Xie Ye is also exhausted, everyone is exhausted. She has traveled with me for so long, had to live on wild plants, been poisoned, hauled stones, and in the end still returned to this life. No one hates the world except me, except me with my world-weary way. I just had begun to want to live when I met the end.

Wenxin, to tell you the truth, those who know me won't stop me; there are still things I want to do. You should not think too much about all this. I am very afraid. But I'm not worth your worries. I am just a little upset because those people who were concerned for me are now just about all gone (except for my family).

Do you remember when we went picking peaches? Those were good times, don't you think?

Cheng
August 1993

Dear Mom and Dad,

We have now returned from America, via Tahiti, to our small island in the sea. With that sudden change of winds, I have a better understanding of people now; I bear no hatred or resentment. To be separated, in the farthest corner of the world, is not easy; that people can be born and be together is the fortunate thing. Whether life is good or bad is really only a state of mind.

Little Chubs is adorable; I thought he would have changed, but he's still the same, except he's much better looking, with big beautiful eyes. He understands things now, and is very lively. When I hold him all my troubles seem to melt away. People really do not understand; yet going through some sort of disaster, one realizes now that flesh and blood are much more important than life's imaginings and fantasies. If one can learn to love what one already possesses, that is a blessing. One cannot expect desires to become reality. In fact, desires will for the most part always be unrealized.

Having just returned home, I'm filled with these sentimental thoughts . . .

Now I can spend everyday with Little Chubs, and I'm learning simple English from him. Sometime in years to come I hope to bring him back home with me. He is smothered with love, but that is because he's such a good boy.

By nature I am not a happy person, but right now I am very much at peace, just playing with Little Chubs and his toy cars . . .

Since we are just back, I'll stop here. The grass is long in the fields, and the little peach trees that I planted before I left are now in bloom. In a few days I'll take some pictures and send them along. Yesterday Little Chubs was playing chess with Emma.[3]

Chubs
October 1993

---

3   The granddaughter of the Maori woman trusted to raise Gu Cheng's son when he was three years old.

Index

A Banner 50
A Crevice 21
A Dark Television 80
A Game 10
A Minor God 126
A Mistake 100
A Narrative 82
A News Item 45
A Prompt 77
A Request for a Painting 79
A Village with No One in It 67
A Warm Summer Day 117
A Wind Blows through the Buildings 65
Above Is Only Sky 107
Accessory to a Crime 84
Accident 108
Adjusting the Frequency 90
After the Air Raid Had Passed 85
Afternoon's Silver Bracelet 95
Against the Current 52
Ah Yes 115
Alert 106
All Those Stories 67
All's Fine 69
Along a Street 12
Aluminum Oxide 119
An Ancient Boat 16
An Evasion 13
Ark 78
Arrow 121
Avant-garde 123
Avoiding Everything 10

Back Bay 155
Back to My Family 177
Baldy Stirs Up Trouble 147
Before Falling to Sleep 88
Beginning of Troubled Times 93
Benighted 118
Between Waiting and Arrival 59
Black Bamboo Park 160
Blood Relatives 90
Book Cover 91
Borders 115
Bridge at Tiger Workshop 167

Bronze Statue 101
Buddha Words 50
Bulin Met a Bandit 39
Bulin's Entry for the Lullaby
    Competition 40
Bulin's Last Instructions 45
Bulin's Military Anti-March 42
Bulin's Military March 42
Bulin's Speech to the National
    Conference of Nursery Schools 40
Burial Song 89
Butterflies 89

Calendar 134
Cars 81
Chair 133
Changping County 163
China Gate 152
Classical Tales from Waiheke Island 143
Clinging Vines 11
Colored Ink 163
Coming Home 4
Confession 66
Copper 193
Cord 106
Cottage 103
Couplet 43
Creditor Rights 91
Crossing the Border 100
Cut and Paste 162

Days Gone By 101
Dee dee da dee da 124
Devices 108
Dharma's Door 120
Discourse on Fish in the Old Temple of
    Shrine Mountain—A Painting 145
Discoveries 38
Discriminations 29
Distant Traveler in the Grasslands 33
Do You Still Remember the River 29
Double Bottle Rocket into the Sky 146
Drifting Drifting 24
Duplicate Names 132
Dusk 1

Dusk, Who Says 34
Dusky Rainbow 135

Early Summer 22
East China Gate 152
Eating at Desert Creek 189
Elephant Street 172
Encounter 94
Eulogy to the World 92
Eyes 103

Fated to Be Together 166
Feng Terrace 165
Fiction 130
Fishing with Torches—A Painting 144
Fishnets Flying through the Sky—A
    Painting 145
Flowers for a Present 170
For a Lost Star 31
For My Grandmother, Now Departed 32
For My Grave 28
From A Birds-Eye View to the Waterline
    53
Funeral Dirge 44

Ganjiakou Neighborhood 170
Gems 99
Ghosts Enter the City—Eight Poems 137
Going to Worship 128
Good Works, Good Discussion 144
Government Street 174
Grass Shack 5
Grasslands 24
Growing Up 78

Hair White as Snowy Skies 146
Half a Peck 109
Hall of Cherishing Benevolence 169
Heaven's Pure Soil 149
Heaven's Will—A Painting 146
Help 110
Here, We Can't Really Get to Know
    Each Other 25
Hidden Moon Alley 174
Holding Still 104
Home • Home 118
Homesick—A Tune 149
Homework 116
Hopes 110
Horned Toad 89
Huicheng Gate 171
Huokou Neighborhood 173

I Dreamt of Fishes 61
I Gather Together Golden Threads of
    Smoke 81
I Hand You All a Knife 116
I'll Be Going Now 47
I'd Rather Die 14
I'm A Cripple 27
Impression 11
In Conjunction 95
In Response to the Times 92
In That Little Village 83
In the Afternoon 94
Inside the Bottle 79
Into a Still Life 62
It Would Seem Bulin Is Dead 44

Just a Bit of Hope 12

Kiddo 155

Lake Country 6
Last Letters 200
Leroy 121
Life's Fantasy, A Tune 1
Liquid Mercury 114
Lord of the Island 143

Mantis Romance—A Fable 75
Manual of Sackcloth Prognostications 111
Martyred 6
Melting Point 99
Men 114
Meridian Gate 153
Middle of the Month 84
Misfortune that Arrives at Its Appointed
    Time 85
Misty Poetry: An Interview 181
Mouth of the River 85
"Movements" 80
My Fantasies 1
My Résumé 14

Names 103
National Gate 170
Nature 91
Near and Far 10
Near the Sea of Dreams 13
New Year's Eve 19
North Street, Altar of the Moon 164

Off to School 107
Offering Comfort 13
Old Days 90
Oman 133

On Occasion 111
On the Left-hand Side of the Dark Night 50
One Generation 3
One Spring Day 47
One's Self 83
Oriental Courtyard 56
Our Descendants 100
Over the Border 101

Painted Foundation 174
Parting Gift 9
Peace Lake 165
Piled 106
Ping'an Neighborhood 167
Pirates at Sea 132
Poetry and Life 189
Poetry Lessons 179
Poetry Stomps Out of My Heart 97
Poster for the New Year 89
Poverty, It Has a Cold Wet Nose 65
Preface to *Nameless Flowers* 179
Primary School 88
Proposal Number 0 43
Puppet 127

Queen on the Coin 93

Rain 24
Red Wheat 120
Red Wine 105
Research 43
Returning Home 21
Rostrum Road 174

Sea Basket Blues 129
Seen 129
Self-confidence 26
Separating 52
September 134
Seven Days 135
Shops at Xinjiekou 160
Sitting Here on Heaven's Steps 68
Six Mile Bridge 161
Smokestacks 1
Smoking 119
Snowman 5
Solar Flare 123
South Pond 155
Spring Has Not Yet Come 25
Spring Pavilion 164
Strewn 76
Summer Outside the Window 51

Sun's Self-Immolation—A Painting 147
Switching Husbands 143

Take This Branch of Blossoms 22
Telex 122
Temple of Earth 168
Temple of Myriad Springs 172
The Ability of the Tree to Swim 77
The Ancient War 26
The Art of Pulling Strings 54
The Bell Tower 169
The Bird of Paradise Gets Its Way—A Painting 145
The Birth and Emigration of Bulin 36
The Book of Songs 128
The Bridge 130
The Capital Theater 157
The Case 110
The City: A Dream Sequence 151
The Coolest of Mornings 56
The Eastern Mausoleum 166
The Emporium 156
The Feel of the Wind 104
The Four Seasons: Preserving Dusk and Dawn 86
The Gaze 131
The Girl and the Raccoon 101
The Great Clearing 109
The Ground 61
The Harvest 23
The Holy Child Descends 98
The Mail 164
The Marble Boat 169
The Market 132
The Oil Painting 160
The Old One 57
The One in the Sunlight 113
The Original Recording of Bulin's Prayer 41
The Palace Museum 159
The Peking Public Library 164
The Polishing Factory 165
The Princess's Tomb 164
The Soul Lives in Lonely Quarters 94
The Sound of a Window Opening 133
The Source 82
The Stone that Did Not Fall to Earth 149
The Temple of Heaven 152
The Very Last Time 27
The Warmth of a Winter Day 12
The Weekend 93
The Wind Has Stolen Our Prize 30
There're Not Many Birds in the Village Now 112

This Deep Dark Ditch 66
This Idiot Gets Engaged 145
This Idiot Proposes 144
Thoroughfare 122
Time 113
Tis 95

Up Early 84
Uprising 81

Victory Gate 154
Village Affairs 128

Walled Dreams, and An Awakening 70
We Go Searching for a Lamp 19
We Live on One Side 97
Welded Heat 63
West Market 173
What There Is to Regret 148
Wheat Fields 130
Whether 114
White Pagoda Temple 168
White Stone Bridge 165

Who Could Have Thought 37
Willow Branches 1
Willow Jar 109
Willow Street 170
Wind Dreams 48
Winged Red Banner 169
With a TV Mounted on the Wall 185
Wolf Pack 91
Words 82
Words 135
Work 69
Writing 113
Writing Brush 105

Xidan Shopping District 159

Year's End 129
Ying'er 194
You and I 3
Youth 78

Zhongguan Neighborhood 162